Marten Julian

Cheltenham
BULLETIN BOOK 2021

Marten Julian 2021 ©
69 Highgate, Kendal,
Cumbria, LA9 4ED

01539 741 007
rebecca@martenjulian.com
www.martenjulian.com

First published in Great Britain 2021

Copyright © Marten Julian
Author has asserted his moral rights

Contributors
Marten Julian
Jodie Standing
Ronan Groome
Ian Carnaby

Edited By
Jodie Standing

Proofreader
Ian Greensill

Cover Design & Layout
Steve Dixon

Cover Image
WBY Horse Racing Photography

Reference material:
The Racing Post, Raceform Interactive & Weatherbys

ISBN 978-1-8382317-6-7
ISSN: 2634-0364

Register for our **free** monthly newsletter
Call Rebecca on 01539 741 007 or **email** rebecca@martenjulian.com

Introduction

Hi there!

I would like to thank you for buying this 42nd edition of the *Cheltenham Bulletin Book*.

It seems quite a while since the days when the *Bulletin Book* was the only guide to Cheltenham on the market. Back then I used to write single-handedly over 30,000 words on a typewriter, relying on a tube of Tipp-Ex to remove any errors.

That was followed by a trip to the local photocopy shop and then a long night binding the pages together before stuffing them in envelopes and hoping that Royal Mail did their bit and got them to my clients before the first day of the meeting! How things have moved on …

I now have a team to help at every stage of the process, headed by my daughter Rebecca who has been with me for over half of those 40 years. She is supported by Jodie, my racing assistant and a contributor to this and our other publications, Steve Dixon, Ian Carnaby, Ronan Groome, Paul Day and Ian Greensill, who sets such a high standard of proofreading.

I want to make a special mention of Jodie, whose contribution to the writing, editing and compiling of this year's edition is inestimable. Without her help I would have struggled. Rebecca has also stepped up to the plate, working through to the early hours in challenging circumstances.

There are just shy of 40,000 words in this *Bulletin Book* so, once again, we have produced a separate publication to cover the handicaps.

This was printed in-house, thereby allowing me a few extra days to assess any fresh information that comes through. It has, of course, been provided for subscribers at no extra cost.

You can listen to my updated news for each day either the night before or by 11.30 each morning of the meeting, when my final selections will be given in the first minute of the message (**0906 150 1555** – cost £1.50 a minute at all times).

Many years ago Rebecca and I planned to stop our *Premium Rate Services*, as we don't agree with the charges, but clients contacted us to say they wanted the flexibility of being able to call as and when suited them.

So instead of stopping it we launched my *Telephone & Text Service* which is the same information on a non-Premium Rate number. We pay the additional telephone line charge and you receive a text message daily. It costs £15 to join for Cheltenham week. Please speak to Rebecca if you wish to take advantage of any other benefits we offer for Cheltenham.

I hope that this year's Cheltenham Festival lives up to our expectations and proves both profitable and enjoyable.

Best of luck and bye for now!

Contents

free blogs & newsletters   **follow** Marten on twitter
www.martenjulian.com   **@martenjulian**

Day One

1.20

Look for horses with recent winning form – 21 of the last 24 winners won last time out. The ratings also offer a clue with five of the last eight winners obtaining a rating of 153 or higher. Not a race for outsiders – only one winner from the last ten returned greater than 10/1.

For some of us the Supreme Novices' Hurdle is the most important race of the Festival.

It clearly lacks the standing of the Champion Hurdle and Gold Cup, but for trainers and people like me, who are in it for the long haul, a win in this opening race of the meeting takes the pressure off in a major way.

I can tell you, after doing this job for almost 50 years, that there is no greater challenge than having to write a preview for the final day of the meeting after enduring three washouts.

Apart from the overwhelming feeling of disappointment, there is the knowledge that hundreds of loyal subscribers will be facing a trial of faith in my judgement, perhaps with long-term consequences.

The question of whether too much of the season revolves around this week in March became the topic of discussion a few weeks ago. Well, from our perspective, I can tell you there are clients who structure their entire year and annual holiday around Cheltenham, with orders for our service coming through as early as the autumn.

Then there is the history of this opening race itself.

Some years it has played host to the Irish 'banker of the week', with stories from days gone by of heavy-hitters cancelling their rooms and taking Tuesday night's ferry back home after things went belly up.

On the other side of the coin some great names have appeared on the race's roll of honour – L'Escargot, Bula, Beacon Light, Golden Cygnet, Brave Inca, Menorah, Douvan and, more recently, Altior and last season Shishkin.

Shishkin, for all his class, actually won in the slowest time in the last 20 years – 4 min 08.20 secs – as opposed to Altior's 3 min 46.00 secs, the quickest time in the same period.

In a year when there are a number of contenders for the week's banker, **Appreciate It** is unlikely to top the list. Much fancied as he will prove to be, Shishkin, Concertista, Chacun Pour Soi, Envoi Allen and Monkfish are currently shorter than him in the betting.

Having said that the seven-year-old brings an unblemished record over hurdles into the race, following a fine second over the course when chasing home Ferny Hollow in last spring's Champion Bumper.

Trainer Willie Mullins, who has won the race six times stretching back to 1995 with Tourist Attraction, says that he is surprised at how much speed the horse has.

Last season his first victory under Rules came in a 2m 4f bumper, having won a point to point in March 2018, but he cruised through to beat Risk Factor in a 2m bumper at Leopardstown five weeks before Cheltenham and he has stretched out well, with a hint of quickening, to win three times this season, the last two at Grade 1 level.

As a half-brother to winners over 2m 6f and 3m, out of a half-sister to a 2m 5f hurdle and chase winner, the son of Jeremy has a distaff line that is strongly biased towards stamina. That's no bad thing with this race as it is always run at a strong pace, with that gruelling climb to the line.

Appreciate It is generally a good jumper – he's a big horse who dwarfs his hurdles – and he has been ridden in his races up with the pace.

Tactically I expect that to be the case here, with the rider probably keen to get a lead before kicking on around the final bend.

Appreciate It had three and a quarter lengths to spare over

Ballyadam at Leopardstown, having had that horse 16 lengths behind him the time before. Paul Townend did say of the winner afterwards that he thought he was not quite at his best, but I view the distances more a reflection on the runner-up's improvement.

This horse has a great cruising speed and covers a lot of ground with his loping stride. He looks a worthy favourite for this race and is a horse with an exciting future, especially over a longer trip.

Ballyadam and Metier are vying for second favourite.

Ballyadam was very highly regarded by former trainer Gordon Elliott last season, atoning for a shock 1/4 defeat on his Rules debut in a bumper at Navan when hacking up by 18 lengths five weeks later at Downpatrick, leaving Jamie Codd singing his praises afterwards.

The switch to hurdling started well, with a very easy success on his seasonal return at Down Royal, followed by a win over Cask Mate in the Grade 1 Royal Bond Hurdle at Fairyhouse. On each occasion he showed a turn of foot despite rattling the top bar of the final flight both times.

A month later he came up against Appreciate It in the Paddy Power Future Champions Novice Hurdle at Leopardstown. Looking out of sorts from an early stage, he didn't have a cut at his hurdles and was held approaching the last before folding tamely on the run-in.

Last time out he narrowed the deficit with Appreciate It down to three and a quarter lengths having jumped with more zest. Enjoying the cover in mid-division, he was always travelling well and turned for home on the bridle looking a serious threat to the favourite before fumbling the final flight, losing momentum but staying on well for second.

Ballyadam would probably not have won anyway, but he showed a turn of foot and – most significantly – seemed very content with the cover of his rivals around him. This augurs well for the big field at Cheltenham.

His former handler won this race with the mercurial Labaik four years ago. Ballyadam is more straightforward but his hurdling is a concern.

Metier, a 90-rated middle-distance performer on the Flat for Irish handler Andrew Slattery, already looks a superior class over hurdles.

Most impressive to the eye when winning a novices' hurdle in heavy ground at Newton Abbot in late October, he then carried his penalty to success in a Class 2 event at Ascot.

Establishing a clear lead from flagfall, he bowled along unthreatened until the second last, when he came away again when challenged by two rivals.

Next time he was raised in class for the Grade 1 Tolworth Hurdle, run in heavy ground at Sandown.

Facing such a stiff test he was held up sixth of the seven runners, moving well throughout and putting up some good leaps down the back straight, before challenging on the bridle approaching the second last and staying on well up the hill to beat Shakem Up'Arry by 12 lengths in a good time.

Regarding Cheltenham he has shown that he can settle and he travels well through a race. One concern is that he has a tendency to lug right over a hurdle and he is untried on ground better than soft. In fact his best form on the Flat came on easy going as well.

Metier probably has a stronger finishing kick than Appreciate It and Ballyadam and he has the best speed figure in the race. He is a very good horse.

Bob Olinger is more likely to run in the Ballymore.

The six-year-old son of Sholokhov gave Ferny Hollow something to think about on his hurdling debut at Gowran Park on heavy ground in November.

The following month he made all to land odds of 1/8 in a 2m 4f maiden hurdle at Navan before beating Blue Lord by six and a half lengths in a Grade 1 contest at Naas.

Bob Olinger is from a family of stayers – his dam is a half-sister to a winner over three miles – but for all his talent I can't see him having the pace to beat the leading contenders in this two-miler.

Soaring Glory put himself forward for the race when winning Newbury's Betfair Hurdle from a mark of 133 by three lengths.

Before that he ran four times over hurdles, winning a Chepstow novices' contest in October and then running second to the useful Dusart at Newbury. He fell two hurdles from home next time at Wetherby before running third to My Drogo in a Grade 2 at Ascot.

The Betfair, in its former incarnations, has proved a stepping stone to the Supreme but the ones that ran well here had higher ratings than Soaring Glory.

Jonjo O'Neill's son of Fame And Glory is a progressive horse but he needs to improve again to beat those above him in the betting.

One of the most intriguing horses in the race is **Dreal Deal**.

Trainer Ronan McNally has expressed concerns about the six-year-old's participation due to an outbreak of aspergillosis in his yard – a reaction caused by mould, possibly resulting from a bad batch of forage.

His presence would certainly add spice to the race, just as it did on the day when he was backed from 20/1 overnight to 6/4 before hacking up from a mark of 84 in a 2m 6f 80-102 handicap hurdle at Navan in September.

He then won four more, twice from marks of 45 and 51 on the Flat and then off 106 and 111 back over hurdles, before defying a market drift to beat Ganapathi in a 2m Grade 2 at Punchestown in January.

The feature of this horse's performances has been the ease with which he moves through a race and the change of gear he can produce at the end of it.

A mark of 145 leaves him 8lb adrift of Appreciate It but we haven't seen the best of this scopey individual and, if he does get to post, then rest assured he has the class to be competitive.

In the longer term he has a big race in him from a mark of 78 on the Flat.

Willie Mullins has expressed uncertainty over the target for **Blue Lord**.

The six-year-old landed a maiden hurdle on his Irish debut at Punchestown in November before running second to Bob Olinger, having pulled hard early on, in a 2m 4f Grade 1 at Naas in January.

He was then third to Appreciate It, beaten six lengths, in the Grade 1 Chanelle Pharma Novice Hurdle at Leopardstown in February.

Although beaten, Blue Lord, who gives his hurdles plenty of air, showed a turn of foot at Leopardstown. The book says he has to reverse the form with the first and second, but I get the feeling this horse has more to offer.

A strongly run two miles looks the right race for him and he is a leading outsider.

Mullins is also likely to call upon **Ganapathi**, who ran fifth last time over 2m 6f in a Grade 1 contest at Leopardstown.

Before that he finished three lengths behind Dreal Deal in the Grade 2 at Punchestown having won a maiden hurdle at Cork in November.

The five-year-old looked sure to win at Punchestown until the winner swept past him after the last. A mark of 137 leaves him more than a stone behind the favourite but he is lightly raced with more to offer.

It requires a leap of faith to believe **Thedevilscoachman** can reverse the almost 20-length deficit with Appreciate It from their meeting at Leopardstown over Christmas. That was the only time Noel Meade's five-year-old has been beaten.

A bumper winner at Naas in January, he started over hurdles in November with a win at Cork and then, after finishing fifth at Leopardstown, he won a novice at Navan and a Listed novice at Punchestown.

The son of Elusive Pimpernel's main asset is his turn of foot.

He quickened in a few strides to win his last two races and, from what I have seen, he has a better turn of foot than the favourite. He does, though, need to be within challenging distance at the last and that run in the Future Champions at Leopardstown reflects the gulf he needs to bridge but, at 20/1, he appeals as one of the race's stronger outsiders. He has an alternative entry in the County Hurdle but the trainer has twice won the Supreme, with Go Native in 2009 and Sausalito Bay in 2000.

Bareback Jack is unbeaten in three starts over hurdles, racing prominently to win novice events twice at Musselburgh and at Catterick.

Donald McCain sent out Cinders And Ashes to win this in 2012 and there is much to like about this son of Getaway. He scurries along in a pleasing manner but needed a shuffle or two from Brian Hughes to get the better of the 133-rated Tommy's Oscar last time out and that form doesn't look good enough for this level.

Gowel Road, rated 131, has plenty to find but there is no doubting his attitude.

A high-spirited horse, who was a handful to break in, he ran second to the talented Bear Ghylls on his hurdling debut in November and was then fourth at Newbury to Good Ball.

He returned to the Berkshire track to win his next two starts, reversing previous form with Good Ball on his most recent start.

Gowel Road is from the family of Mister Morose and he has that tenacity which can be a hallmark of horses trained by Nigel Twiston-Davies, who won this with Arctic Kinsman in 1994. He could run well, especially if the ground rides on the easy side.

Others that warrant a mention are **Keskonrisk**, a staying-on third to Appreciate It at Leopardstown, triple hurdle winner **Benson**, who then ran on steadily to finish fourth to Not So Sleepy off 137 at Ascot and **Haut En Couleurs**, a winner in France and yet to run for Willie Mullins.

Conclusion

Appreciate It is a worthy favourite on form but he could be vulnerable to a rival with a turn of foot. Mind you that assumes there is anything near enough to mount a challenge approaching the last.

I have been keen on Ballyadam for a while but he may be better suited to a less galloping track.

Metier has strong claims and is still unexposed but the two I like are Blue Lord, who has other options at the meeting, and Gowel Road. The latter may prefer soft ground, which looks unlikely. They are available at 16/1 and 25/1 respectively.

Of the two I favour Blue Lord.

Blue Lord (Gowel Road)

The Sporting Life Arkle Challenge Trophy Steeple Chase (Grade 1) *abt 2m*	1.55

Not a great race for Paul Nicholls – of his 13 runners, only Azertyuiop was successful and the remainder were unplaced. Another race where recent winning form is important – 16 of the last 20 winners won last time out. Look at horses rated 160+ – six have won from just 12 runners since 2012.

Nicky Henderson and Willie Mullins, the two top trainers in Cheltenham Festival history, have ten Arkle wins between them and hold the top two in the market for this year's renewal. It's very likely one of the pair will elongate their good record in the two-mile novice chase championship, or could Dan Skelton issue another signal of intent by gaining a Grade 1 Festival breakthrough?

Let's start with **Shishkin**. Where else? The son of Sholokhov has been favourite for this contest ever since he defied significant interference in running to win last season's Supreme Novices' Hurdle.

Nicky Henderson's gelding went into the race off the back of just two runs over hurdles (technically three but fell early first time out) and was notably weak in the betting beforehand. The interference he suffered came as the result of the right-jumping tendencies of the same owners' Asterion Forlonge, who caused the fall of Elixir D'ainay and Captain Guinness at the flight coming down the hill, with Shishkin hampered as a result. It should have been a case of 'race over' from there, but Nico De Boinville was able to work him back into the race, and that was very impressive. In the end he just held off Abacadabras, a Grade 1 winner over hurdles in Ireland this season, with the pair of them well clear.

That marked him out as an above average Supreme winner and he has done nothing this season to suggest he can't, at the very least, be as good a chaser as he was a hurdler with a couple of Grade 2 wins at Kempton and Doncaster, having earlier won his novice chase at the former.

If you were picky, and you can afford to be in a race like this year's Arkle, you could point to the overall strength of Shishkin's chase form. Well, at least you could have until last weekend. Prior to that his comfortable defeat of the 149-rated Eldorado Allen, a Grade 2 winner earlier in the season, looked the pick of the bunch, but Tamaroc Du Mathan, a well held second to him in the Wayward Lad, was an impressive winner of the Grade 2 Pendil Novices' Chase at Kempton. That Paul Nicholls-trained horse travelled beautifully and comfortably held the 150-rated Ga Law, a useful yardstick for novice chase form this year.

For me, that solidifies the Shishkin case. The strength of his form was an area of concern for some, but that Tamaroc Du Mathan performance was in the mould of a low 150s horse – for all that he may have progressed – and Shishkin had beaten him easily. It was also noticeable in the Wayward Lad that when Gumball tried to lead him, he paid the price heavily, trailing in a 30-length last of four.

Shishkin's jumping has been immaculate and the times of his races more than suggest he is well up to Grade 1 standard. The closing argument and the most crucial aspect to his profile, especially against his two main market rivals is that he has the Cheltenham know-how that they don't – Grade 1 Festival form, and that is very significant. He is the correct favourite.

In contrast to Shishkin, who was well established through his Festival heroics prior to this season, **Energumene** has come from nowhere. He won his only start over hurdles impressively last season but given that win came at Gowran Park in March, it probably went a little under the radar with Cheltenham in full focus.

He returned to the Kilkenny track for his chase debut in November and could hardly have been more impressive in an 18-length win from the front, recording a time that compared extremely well with other races over the same distance on the card. That victory came over two and a half miles, but so good was his jumping, his trainer Willie Mullins felt he should use that strength where it would be more pertinent, back over a two-mile trip and Energumene answered that call emphatically – first proving much too strong for Captain Guinness at Naas and then when completely outclassing a Grade 1 field in the Irish Arkle at Leopardstown.

Both of those runs were from the front and at Leopardstown, a top class field simply couldn't go with him. He beat stablemate Franco De Port into second, and he had won the Grade 1 novice chase at the same track over Christmas, so it looks really solid form, with the likes of Felix Desjy and Darver Star unable to live with the punishing pace, and beaten long distances. The win compared nicely in terms of time with Chacun Pour Soi's Dublin Chase win earlier on the card.

If you were to pick at Energumene, he did jump to his right at Leopardstown, particularly down the back straight. While that proved no hindrance to him in the end, it will be more difficult to get away with that against a top-form Shishkin. But, he probably has achieved more than that rival in form terms over fences this term, and if acting at Cheltenham, he can put it up to the Henderson horse.

Allmankind blazed a trail as a juvenile hurdler last season and he has stayed true to his tearaway tactics over fences this term. Having begun the season over hurdles (trying to concede weight all around in a conditions event at Cheltenham), he was quickly switched to fences where he scored by 13 lengths on his debut and then went on to see off a similarly exciting type in Hitman, the pair of them miles clear of their rivals, in the usually informative Henry VIII Novices' Chase at Sandown.

Allmankind ran that race in a faster time than Politologue ran when impressively landing the Tingle Creek later on the card, although the son of Sea The Moon did carry 11lbs less, given he had a four-year-olds' allowance. Nevertheless that was an impressive time and he showed that he had progressed past the need of that allowance when he won the Kingmaker Novices' Chase at Warwick recently, when on this occasion he had to concede weight to the much improved, 152-rated Sky Pirate, who made mistakes when trying to keep up with him.

Five-year-olds have a good record in the Arkle though they probably need to be very good – Well Chief and Voy Por Ustedes were the last two winners in 2004 and 2006, although Fakir D'oudairies went close when second to Put The Kettle On last season. He should win the battle for the lead with Energumene and the question will be can he draw mistakes from his main two rivals without impairing his own jumping.

It's probably unfair to draw a comparison to the way his season went last term – impressive in three starts prior to Cheltenham but ultimately found out in the Triumph – and suggest something similar may happen, given he has shown himself to be an excellent novice chaser racing against horses older than him. However it is still a slight concern in what is a vintage Arkle.

Bar the top three, it's 16/1 next best and it may be that we have a six or seven-runner field. With that in mind, **Franco De Port** makes some appeal. As mentioned, he won the Grade 1 Racing Post Novice Chase at Christmas and I think he did well to finish second to Energumene in the Irish equivalent of this race. He made a bad mistake at the fence just before the back straight and got shuffled back and he was also impaired by the fall of Captain Guinness at the second last.

This race screams pace up front and his hold-up style, implemented very well by Bryan Cooper this season, is well suited to pick up the pieces late on and it wouldn't be a surprise at all to see him grab a place.

I wouldn't give up completely on **Captain Guinness**. He was travelling well when taken out by the fall of Elixir D'ainay in the Supreme last season and though he was pulled up early on his chasing debut, he got his season back on track with an easy win in his beginners chase at Punchestown before finding Energumene too hot at Naas.

He wasn't done with when he came down at the second last at Leopardstown and though his jumping is an area of significant concern, he undoubtedly has an engine, and seemed to handle Cheltenham's undulations fine until his race was ended prematurely last season.

Fusil Raffles is three from four over fences and two of those wins have come at Cheltenham, one over the Arkle distance, but is reported to be heading up in trip for the Marsh.

Conclusion

This is potentially one of the races of the Festival, and any of the top three in the market could have been clear favourite in an average year. I think it comes down to Shishkin's Cheltenham form – he is proven in the white heat of a Festival race and while Energumene may well have no problems on the course, we simply can't be sure of it yet. The slight tendency to jump right would also worry me for the Mullins horse, and I think tactically this could set up nicely for Shishkin, with Nico De Boinville able to stalk his main two front-running rivals from behind. Of the remainder, Franco De Port is a horse I like a lot. He should be suited by the extra stamina test Cheltenham presents and could run on for a place late in the day. (Ronan)

Shishkin (Franco De Port)

The Unibet Champion Hurdle Challenge Trophy (Grade 1)
2m abt ½f

3.05

Winning form is important here – the last six winners were unbeaten that season. Nicky Henderson and Willie Mullins are the two trainers to follow here. Between them, they have won nine of the last 12 renewals.

The debate about the mares' allowance – they receive 7lb from the geldings here – will regather its momentum if either Epatante or Honeysuckle should win this Champion Hurdle.

The odds are quite short that one of them will, as they are first and second in the betting, but perhaps more than that I envisage this becoming a race that could be won or lost on tactics.

In brief I see the race run as follows.

Epatante will be held up to produce her turn of foot. Honeysuckle will be up with the pace and then kick on, perhaps, turning for home. Goshen seemed more relaxed at Wincanton, so may be held up and produced late. Abacadabras and Sharjah will definitely be held up, possibly until after the last. Silver Streak may try to make all, given the success of that tactic at Kempton, while Aspire Tower will be prominent, possibly from flagfall.

In my view Aspire Tower is the most likely to win the battle for the early lead.

The one thing that looks assured is that the gallop will be fast and furious, and that could set things up for a closer and the obvious beneficiary in that event is **Epatante**.

Two seasons ago Nicky Henderson's mare retired for the summer having won novice hurdles at Kempton and Exeter, concluding her campaign with a mediocre ninth of 22 in the Mares' Novices' Hurdle here – a performance many pounds below Champion Hurdle class.

Before joining Henderson she had won twice in France, a bumper and then a Grade 1 bumper over an extended 1m 4f on heavy ground at Saint-Cloud in November 2017.

In fairness, the trainer did report in a pre-season stable preview that the mare might have been adversely affected at the 2019 Cheltenham Festival by her flu jab, having initially thought beforehand that she was the stable's best chance of a winner.

He went on to suggest that handicaps would be the plan, and she duly started the campaign in a 0-155 Listed handicap at Newbury in November from a mark of 137. Keen throughout the race, as was the case in the past, she was a little hesitant over the hurdles – notably over the second last – but came away on the run to the line to win by six lengths.

Just under a month later she went to Kempton for the Grade 1 Christmas Hurdle, attracting strong late support down to 2/1 co-favourite.

Once again she was keen, despite getting plenty of cover, but this time she jumped more efficiently – notably gaining an advantage with a spirited leap at the third last. Cruising through and travelling powerfully on the turn for home, she was delivered with a challenge between the last two flights and surged away on the run-in to beat

Silver Streak by five lengths, with her stable companion, Verdana Blue, in fourth.

This was both impressive to the eye and impressive on the book. Her jumping was better than at Newbury as was the turn of foot she produced. Furthermore, in second was the reliable Silver Streak, with useful performers stretched out behind.

Her jumping in the Champion Hurdle, for which she was equipped with earplugs, was slick in the main. She clipped the top of a couple of flights and snatched at the third last, but she never lost momentum and travelled smoothly throughout the course of the race.

Produced with a challenge at the last, she put in one of her best leaps of the race and found a change of gear to pull away and beat Sharjah by three lengths.

She became the fifth of her sex to win the Champion Hurdle, giving Nicky Henderson his eighth winner of the race and owner, JP McManus, his fourth in a row.

This season started very well, with a facile defeat of the talented Sceau Royal in the Fighting Fifth under a ride of supreme confidence from Aidan Coleman. The turn of foot she showed after the last there was impressive.

Things didn't go according to plan next time in the Christmas Hurdle, where a mistake three from home seemed to unsettle her. A little hesitant at the first, she was big at the second, better at the third and fourth, good at the fifth, clouted the sixth and was then fine over the last two.

To my eyes she didn't look quite herself from flagfall, never travelling with the ease we have come to expect of her. The trainer says she was subsequently found to have a sore back, which has since been treated.

Given the likelihood that her main threats will be up with the pace, Aidan Coleman will have something to aim at. He will know that if she is back to her best it is highly unlikely there will be anything to match her change of gear.

Her challenge will, though, require precision timing.

Nicky Henderson hopes that **Buveur D'Air** can return to his best for the big day.

He had time off after sustaining an injury in last season's Fighting Fifth Hurdle, when a wedge of hurdle stuck in his hoof. There followed a complicated procedure to extricate it, necessitating a piece of his hoof being cut away.

He was handled with great sensitivity by Nico De Boinville on his return at Haydock in January. Delivered to challenge between the last two, he was considerately nudged along to the line without his rider asking too much of him, understandably given his recent history.

A faller in the race in the Champion Hurdle of 2019, he won the race in 2017 and 2018. The winner of 17 of his 25 races under Rules, the feature of Buveur D'Air's career has been his slick jumping. He is lightning quick over a hurdle which, with his ability to change gear, have combined to make him an awesome performer.

He has also displayed, when required, an admirable willingness to put his head down and battle. This was never more apparent than when he just got the better of Melon in this race in 2018 after looking beaten halfway up the run-in.

He is now a 10-year-old but that is no barrier to winning hurdling's crown – the great Sea Pigeon was that age when he won the race for the first time in 1980 before following up a year later at the age of 11.

Furthermore, Buveur D'Air is a 'young' 10-year-old, in so much as he has raced just 25 times over seven years of racing.

His current price of 25/1 borders on the disrespectful, and there will be plenty of people kicking themselves if he wins at such long odds.

The likely favourite is **Honeysuckle**, unbeaten in 10 starts under Rules and winner of her sole point-to-point where she beat the talented Annie Mc, now rated on 149 over fences, by 15 lengths. With the benefit of hindsight that was some performance from such an inexperienced horse.

She won four times in the 2018/19 season, progressing from a maiden through to Listed, Grade 3 and then Grade 1 company over 2m 4f, the feature on each occasion being an ability to surge away from the opposition between the last two flights of hurdles.

She made further progress last season, beating the males in the Grade 1 Hatton's Grace in December and then showing that she had the tenacity to match her talent when holding the late run of Darver Star, after a tussle with Petit Mouchoir, back at two miles in the Irish Champion Hurdle.

The Champion Hurdle was a serious consideration last spring but connections eventually opted for the Mares' Hurdle over 2m 4f.

Up against Benie Des Dieux, who was rated 4lb superior, she was ridden handy throughout and her rider, Rachael Blackmore, enterprisingly shot her through a gap on the rails on the home turn to seize an advantage which stood her in good stead on the run to the line.

This season she started with a half-length defeat of Ronald Pump in the Hatton's Grace, sticking her neck out bravely to hold the runner-up's late challenge on the run-in.

She moved to yet another level when she dropped back to two miles for the Irish Champion Hurdle in February.

Close up throughout she settled comfortably on the outside of the field travelling smoothly with her head, as usual, bowed low until the third last, where she moved up alongside the pacesetting Petit Mouchoir.

It was then that her rider allowed her to stride on, by the second last five lengths clear, and turning for home she held that advantage over the improving Abacadabras, passing the line 10 lengths clear of the runner-up.

The race was run in a good time – 2.6 seconds faster than the handicapper in the next, who carried a stone less weight. Her jumping was slick and efficient, having at times been a little slipshod in the past.

Honeysuckle is the sort of mare that warms the heart. She is versatile regarding trip, appears to handle all types of ground and has shown that she can battle.

Top form over two and a half miles can be of great benefit in a Champion Hurdle and her rider will be keen to exploit her stamina, mindful of Epatante's turn of foot.

The likely strong pace will help in that respect but her rider will need to approach the race with an open mind. The time to decide when to kick will be critical.

Goshen is hard to assess.

His last-flight departure when a long-looking 10 lengths clear in the Triumph Hurdle left backers in despair, although subsequent observation absolved the jockey from blame with the horse's left-hind hoof somehow planting itself on his left-fore hoof, briefly sticking and causing him to trip and unseat his rider.

One can never be certain of such things, especially when the climb up the hill at Cheltenham is a factor, but Goshen would probably have won by at least 10 lengths.

He did little to restore the faith of followers when beaten twice on the Flat in the autumn – off 88 – and then finishing last of 10 behind Song For Someone in the International Hurdle at Cheltenham in December.

After that disappointment Gary Moore took matters into his own hands, riding Goshen himself "around the countryside" to give him a change of scenery.

I expressed a concern when previewing this race in my *Dark Horses* that his trailblazing style of racing may not lend itself to winning a Champion Hurdle but that may be unfounded.

Make A Stand made all to win the race in 1997, since when Faugheen and Annie Power have also won the race from the front.

Yet what we saw last time out at Wincanton was a more relaxed and mentally mature horse.

Still a little keen, but not uncontrollably so, he jumped adequately throughout and it was clear leaving the back straight that Jamie Moore had an awful lot of horse under him. His rider allowed him to go two lengths clear of Navajo Pass and he then drew further away to win hard held, still on the bridle passing the post.

The time was comfortably the fastest of the three races run over the distance that day, while the form stands up to the closest inspection.

The winner reversed a 29-length beating from the time before at Cheltenham with the runner-up while Navajo Pass was 41 lengths back in third having beaten Buveur D'Air at Haydock.

What pleased the trainer most of all was that he won "without having to be asked, he just ran". He came out in good spirits on the following Monday.

Goshen handles heavy ground but it was no worse than soft at last year's Festival and as a son of Authorized I would expect him to be well suited to quicker going.

The likely strong pace will help Goshen relax while his rider now knows, from Wincanton, that he doesn't need to be at the head of affairs.

Many people would love to see Goshen win this race, not only for the Moore family but also to atone for last year's misfortune.

But there is no collateral form to work from unless you assume he would have won the Triumph by a wide margin. If so, then he has the beating of Aspire Tower, Allmankind and Navajo Pass, who finished second, third and fourth.

Aspire Tower has beaten Abacadabras this season and chased home Sharjah, while Allmankind is a top-flight novice chaser with the Arkle in his sights. Navajo Pass was a long way behind Goshen at Wincanton.

Perhaps the last word should be left to the trainer. Gary Moore has worked his fingers to the bone to overcome the challenges of this most demanding profession, managing to father a dynasty in the process, and he has said for a while now that Goshen is something special.

Whether he had been aware of that when the horse was racing at two, his three defeats earning him a mark of just 64 which rose to 88 following a hat-trick of successes as a three-year-old, is for the man who pays the bills to know!

The best has yet to come from **Abacadabras**.

Fourth to Envoi Allen in the 2019 Weatherbys Champion Bumper and then runner-up to Colreevy in the Grade 1 bumper at Punchestown, his career over hurdles began with victories at Gowran Park and Navan, overcoming a few sloppy jumps in the process, before chasing home old rival Envoi Allen in the Royal Bond Novice Hurdle at Fairyhouse in December.

That was followed by a comfortable defeat of Heaven Help Us in the Paddy Power Future Champions Novice Hurdle at Leopardstown before going down by a head to Shishkin in the Supreme Novices' Hurdle at Cheltenham, where he was possibly unlucky after being hampered by a faller at the penultimate flight from home.

Slowly away there, he soon made up the lost ground and he was perfectly poised to challenge when he was hampered, losing momentum, by the incident between Elixir D'ainay and Captain Guinness at the second last. He was soon back on the bridle and looked the likely winner jumping the last until caught close home by Shishkin, finishing 11 lengths clear of Chantry House in third. Afterwards, his trainer said the horse was probably left in front too soon.

This season opened with an odds-on defeat in a Grade 2 at Down Royal, beaten four and a half lengths by Aspire Tower after a hesitant round of jumping. He again jumped sketchily when beating Saint Roi by a neck in the Morgiana Hurdle at Punchestown before running down the field in the Grade 1 Matheson Hurdle at Leopardstown, following which he was found to have mucus in his trachea.

He then ran his best race of the season when a 10-length second to Honeysuckle in the Irish Champion Hurdle.

On paper, the son of Davidoff has valid claims but the concern is his hurdling technique. He often loses momentum over the obstacles and a year out of his novice season he still gets the odd one wrong.

Yet Abacadabras has a number of things going for him.

The first is the prospect of good ground – his action suggests he would be well suited to it and the trainer agrees. The second is that he ran the best race of his life here last season, just getting caught by a top-class performer. The third is that he ran the best race of his season last time out. Finally he will love the strong pace.

I have a strong feeling that we're going to see this horse run a very good race.

Silver Streak would be a popular winner for Evan Williams.

The winner of eight of his 32 starts, he has performed consistently well at the highest level, notably here at Cheltenham. Third to Espoir D'Allen in this race two years ago, his best subsequent performance came last time at Kempton, when he made all to beat Epatante by six and a half lengths in the Christmas Hurdle.

Excuses were made for the runner-up that day – probably with some justification – but he is now rated 7lb better than when he ran in this race two years ago and has every right to be in the field.

I can't find a valid reason why Silver Streak should not go close to winning the Champion Hurdle. He loves the track, having run second three times and third once from five starts here, and the figures show he is better than ever. He likes good ground but tactics may be a problem.

Clearly well suited by making the running at Kempton, it won't be easy to adopt the same tactics around here at this level. He doesn't need to dominate, but there will be a great temptation to do so after last time.

The favourite to set the pace is **Aspire Tower**. That has been the case in each of his six starts over hurdles, ridden on each occasion by Rachael Blackmore, who now rides Honeysuckle.

Aspire Tower's best run came in defeat last time at Leopardstown, where he ran second to Sharjah in the Grade 1 Matheson Hurdle. The time before was back in October, when he made all to beat Abacadabras in a Grade 2 at Down Royal.

Last season ended with a second to Burning Victory in the Triumph Hurdle where, of course, Goshen held a commanding lead until the last-flight mishap.

Henry de Bromhead believes Aspire Tower was below his best there, jumping sketchily and to his left through the race. He had fallen at the last on his previous start at Leopardstown and the trainer says the season "might have caught up with him" at Cheltenham.

I can't imagine Aspire Tower managing to maintain his gallop through to the line. He is, though, a genuine enough performer and he will give his backers a run for their money.

Supporters of **Sharjah** will argue that 16/1 is a fair price for a horse beaten just two lengths in the race last year.

I had given Sharjah a strong chance in the 2019 Champion Hurdle but he was brought down by the fall of Buveur D'Air at the third flight.

Last season was mixed, with a disappointing first run behind stable companion Saldier at Punchestown followed by a defeat of Petit Mouchoir in a Grade 1 at Leopardstown over Christmas. He quickened up well on that occasion but in his race before Cheltenham he again disappointed, dropping away to finish sixth of nine to Honeysuckle.

He left that form far behind in the Champion Hurdle, jumping slickly in arrears and travelling well as the field approached the home turn. Poised to challenge, he jumped the last with every chance but could not match the winner's turn of foot, staying on well to finish three and three-quarter lengths ahead of the third, Darver Star.

Sharjah takes some knowing so the absence of his regular rider Patrick Mullins, due to the restrictions, is not ideal. He does, though, have a sharp change of gear and he is yet another horse in the field that will be tailgating on the turn for home.

The prospect of good ground could see **Verdana Blue** in the line-up.

The eight-year-old has an alternative target in the Mares' Hurdle, but she ran a cracker on softer ground than ideal when third from a mark of 102 in the Ebor and the 100/1 available in a place for her at the time of writing is too big.

Stable companion **Buzz** ran well at the weights in the Betfair Hurdle to finish fifth but latest news is that the Coral Cup is the preferred option.

The enigma of the race is **James Du Berlais**, about whom we know very little.

Bought by Simon Munir and Isaac Souede, probably for a lot of money, he is now with Willie Mullins having been trained in France by Robert Collet.

From what we can glean he has become a very consistent horse, with a run of form reading 212-121212 all at Listed or Graded level. Each of those runs came on ground described as very soft, or heavy, and each race was over 2m 2f or further.

I have seen a couple of his races, which show him to be a slick jumper with a strong finish. He ended last season as the third-highest-rated four-year-old in France behind Nirvana Du Berlais and For Fun. He was bought to be a novice chaser but the concern will be the ground.

The market will give us a clue to stable expectations but regardless of how he runs he is clearly a horse of great talent, with a future over fences next season.

Conclusion

I have played this race through many times in my mind and I never get the same result.

The first thing to say is that I don't think there is any horse with a clear-cut edge over the others. The form book suggests that is the case and it's a race that could be won more as a consequence of enterprise from the saddle than core ability.

Honeysuckle was my selection in the Dark Horses, *but she will need to seize a clear advantage on the run to the line if she is to hold the late pouncers. Of these Epatante has the most potent turn of foot but Abacadabras and Sharjah will be trying to do the same.*

Then we have Goshen. Is he good enough? And if so, how will he be ridden? What we do know is that he appeared to be back to his best at Wincanton while Epatante has to be forgiven her last run at Kempton.

James Du Berlais is one to watch with a view to the future and we mustn't forget Buveur D'Air, who has been here and done it – twice. Verdana Blue will have her backers at 100/1 if the ground is reasonable.

I have, after much deliberation, opted for Goshen. I am not enamoured of his price – 4/1 seems very short against the two mares – but he is the one that left a tingle down my spine when he won at Wincanton.

He may need to be special to win this, but he just could be. (Marten)

Goshen (Honeysuckle)

The Close Brothers Mares' Hurdle Race (Grade 1)
2m abt 4f

3.40

A good race for raiders from the Emerald Isle – 11 of the last 13 winners were trained in Ireland. Willie Mullins is the obvious trainer to follow – he has won nine of the last 13 renewals. Winning distance also offers a clue – 12 of the last 13 winners had won over 2m 4f or further.

Most people expect Ireland to dominate the Cheltenham Festival and it is easy enough to understand their confidence. Raiders from across the Irish Sea have standout chances in many of the top races and are strongly represented in the handicaps as well.

As far as the Grade 1 Close Brothers Mares' Hurdle on the opening day is concerned, Willie Mullins saddles hot favourite **Concertista** with every chance of improving still further his phenomenal record in the race.

Put simply, Mullins can win this event almost for fun. Few will have forgotten Quevega and Benie Des Dieux, while in Concertista he has the sort of improving mare more than capable of dominating for a while.

Concertista is owned by Simon Munir and Isaac Souede. Her form on the level in France was modest, indeed she won only one of her six races and that was in the provinces. But, as with so many horses trained by Mullins, she has proved a revelation over jumps. Remarkably, she was making her hurdles debut for the trainer – after a racecourse absence of 620 days – when finishing second at 66/1 in the Dawn Run Mares' Novices' Hurdle, beaten a short head by stable companion Eglantine Du Seuil, in 2019. Victory in a maiden hurdle looked a formality after that but the following season she was beaten twice before finishing third in a valuable mares' handicap hurdle at Leopardstown.

That was all Concertista needed to spark her campaign and this time she was hugely impressive at Cheltenham in the mares' novices' hurdle, going one better than the previous year and pulling a dozen lengths clear of Dolcita in the hands of Daryl Jacob. Typically, Mullins has brought her on steadily but relentlessly this term, winning the Grade 2 Irish Stallion Farms Hurdle at Fairyhouse and the Grade 3 Advent Insurance Mares' Hurdle at Leopardstown after Christmas. In the first of those two races, following an absence of 261 days, she beat Minella Melody quite tidily but in the second she stretched the winning margin to six and a half lengths, scoring most impressively. Mullins set her aside for Cheltenham after that.

She was almost certain to start favourite for the Mares' Hurdle and 6/5 has been quoted recently, with many serious players unlikely to be put off by the cramped price. Given that the trip is perfect for her, the only word of caution concerns the ground. Concertista has invariably encountered soft conditions over hurdles and, whilst it is unlikely that the word 'firm' will appear in the going description, it's worth keeping an eye on the forecast. And, of course, they still have to jump round, as those who suffered over Benie Des Dieux two years ago will ruefully agree.

In all other respects, Concertista looks highly likely to contribute to the Irish tally.

There has been much talk about the right race for the unbeaten **Honeysuckle** and it looks as if the Champion Hurdle will be the choice. Trainers are seldom (if ever) swayed by media opinion and the general desire to see this hugely talented mare taking on the boys would make little impression on Henry de Bromhead if he thought she had a much better chance in the Mares' Hurdle.

Her prospects in the Champion Hurdle are discussed in the relevant essay and all one can do here is assess her credentials if the trainer opts for the longer race. She won it last year, of course, just denying Benie Des Dieux and that is excellent form. She again underlined her effectiveness over two and a half miles in the Baroneracing.com Hatton's Grace Hurdle at Fairyhouse in November. De Bromhead had left plenty to work on because Honeysuckle just edged home from Ronald Pump with nothing to spare. Allowed to start at 10/11 in the Chanelle Pharma Irish Champion Hurdle at Leopardstown after that, she cruised home by ten lengths from Abacadabras, quite possibly booking her place in the big one at Cheltenham. Maybe De Bromhead thinks avoiding a rival as talented as Concertista is sensible anyway, though he didn't sidestep Benie Des Dieux. Wherever she goes, Honeysuckle will be trying for a perfect dozen, 12 wins out of 12. A truly remarkable mare.

The chief beneficiary when Benie Des Dieux came to grief in 2019 was, of course, Dan Skelton's **Roksana**, who kept on well to hold two more Mullins-trained mares, Stormy Ireland and Good Thyne Tara.

At Kempton recently Skelton seemed to favour the Mares' Hurdle again unless the ground comes up good or good to soft in the Stayers'. It seems a very sound decision, although Roksana has little chance with Honeysuckle on the book, having been left over ten lengths behind in fourth when the latter fought out the finish with Benie Des Dieux last year. She qualifies for the mares' allowance in the Stayers' but was only third to former champion Paisley Park in the Grade 1 Porsche Long Walk Hurdle at Ascot this season before winning a sub-standard Grade 2 Matchbook Betting Podcast Mares' Hurdle quite impressively at the same track last time. Perhaps unfairly, there is the feeling that Roksana is always an each-way proposition, likely to find one or two too good at Grade 1 level.

Nicky Henderson has never won the Mares' Hurdle. He has chances with Dame De Compagnie and Verdana Blue this time, the pair both offering each-way possibilities in the ante-post lists.

Dame De Compagnie is quite a Cheltenham specialist, having run five of her nine races there since arriving from France. She cannot have been easy to train, with long absences between races the rule rather than the exception. When she reappeared this season it was in a novices' chase at Ayr (heavy), where she beat Cornerstone Lad easily enough in a match. Set a very stiff task in the Virgin Bet Scilly Isles Novices' Chase at Sandown (heavy again), she unseated Nico De Boinville when badly hampered by a faller at the 12th.

Dame De Compagnie has plenty to do in the Mares' Hurdle but, on her most recent visit to Cheltenham for last year's Festival, she landed the Coral Cup as a well-backed 5/1 favourite. She was rated 140 over hurdles at that stage but is on 148 now, only 5lb below

Concertista. Also, quite apart from the Henderson factor, never to be underestimated, she has won three of those five races at the course. If readjusting satisfactorily to the smaller obstacles she has to have a chance, but her career path thus far has not been the smoothest.

Verdana Blue once accounted for dual champion hurdler Buveur D'Air in the Grade 1 Christmas Hurdle at Kempton. That was back in 2018 and she went on to finish a creditable fifth in the Champion Hurdle before easily winning the Scottish version at Ayr. A versatile mare, she was fourth in the Sagaro Stakes at Ascot to Derby runner-up Dee Ex Bee and returned there last summer to finish second in the Ascot Stakes before a highly creditable third in the Ebor at York.

Hard to assess this season, she ran three times over hurdles before Christmas and was not disgraced when second to the tough and consistent Silver Streak in the Listed TV Hurdle at Kempton. A disappointing 5/6 favourite when no match for Mrs Hyde in the bet365 Mares' Hurdle at Wetherby, she was unsuited by the wholly unsatisfactory Unibet International Hurdle at Cheltenham, where the last two hurdles were omitted, and her modest eighth is best ignored.

Not seen since then, she will not want the ground drying right out and has plenty to find. However, she has bits and pieces of form at a high level under both codes. Whether she can reproduce it here is very hard to say.

At the time of writing, the bookmakers were going 20/1 bar the horses mentioned so far, including the former Gordon Elliott-trained **Black Tears**. Second to Dame De Compagnie in the Coral Cup, Black Tears was conceding 4lb and would meet her at levels here. A relatively routine Grade 3 victory at Punchestown in the Quevega Mares' Hurdle just before the Festival showed her well-being. Third in Listed and Grade 3 contests before that, Black Tears was beaten a nose and 12 lengths by Buildmeupbuttercup and **Elimay** in the former, the Listed Frontline Security Grabel Mares' Hurdle at Punchestown. She would have little chance with Elimay on that running but bookmakers offer big prices about the pair, there being no obvious reason why Willie Mullins would need Elimay with Concertista heading the market.

His **Great White Shark**, successful in the Cesarewitch at Newmarket last October, is arguably more interesting. Inclined to run too freely when only seventh over three miles in the Grade 2 John Mulhern Galmoy Hurdle at Gowran after that, she missed Black Tears' Punchestown race mentioned above.

Henderson has another possible contender in **Floressa,** who finished only a fair ninth in the Daylesford Mares' Novices' Hurdle at Cheltenham, the race registered as the Dawn Run. Successful in the Listed Intermediate Hurdle at Newbury last autumn, she was only fourth of five in the Grade 1 Christmas Hurdle at Kempton and lost out to Miranda in the Grade 2 Yorkshire Rose Mares' Hurdle at Doncaster. All of Floressa's runs to date have been over two miles or thereabouts. She is not bound to get two and a half in this company.

If Honeysuckle heads for the Champion Hurdle, Henry de Bromhead may run **Minella Melody** here. She is becoming expensive to follow, however, following her unaccountably poor unplaced effort (at 11/4 favourite) in the Grade 2 Mares' Novices' Hurdle a year ago, with three seconds this term, two of them behind Concertista. There is no apparent reason for the form to be reversed.

Of the rest, Paul Webber's **Indefatigable**, not the most reliable but a surprise winner of the Martin Pipe Conditional Jockeys' Handicap Hurdle here last year, may outrun odds of 33/1. She has been out of sorts lately but, on her best form, is not a million miles away from this level.

Conclusion

If Honeysuckle goes for the Champion Hurdle, Willie Mullins' Concertista looks the most likely winner of this race. Her trainer has a tremendous record and Concertista has the perfect profile. Previous winner Roksana may well run into a place.

Of his various other 'possibles', Mullins' Great White Shark is interesting and Paul Webber's Indefatigable may have saved her best for this meeting, as she did last year. (Ian)

Concertista

The National Hunt Steeple Chase Challenge Cup (Amateur Riders' Novices' Steeple Chase) (Grade 2) 3m abt 6f

4.50

Fence experience is a good indicator when trying to find the winner – eight of the last 11 winners had run at least five times over fences. A previous run at the Festival could also prove key with seven of the last 11 winners having experience. Look for horses rated 142 or more.

Former trainer, Gordon Elliott, boasts an unrivalled record in this race having saddled four winners from just eight runners over the past decade starting with Chicago Grey in 2011, which was then followed by Cause Of Causes in 2015, Tiger Roll in 2017 and the ten-year-old, Ravenhill, 12 months ago.

Until recently he trained this year's favourite, the Ronnie Bartlett-owned **Galvin**, whose silks were carried to success in 2018 by Rathvinden.

Just touched off in last year's Northern Trust Company Novices' Handicap Chase behind Imperial Aura, the seven-year-old then went on to win three chases on the bounce back in Ireland, twice at Killarney over 2m 5f, beating Make My Heart Fly by 22 lengths in July before returning a month later for a cosy one-and-a-half length success over Waitnsee. That was followed with a Grade 3 victory at Tipperary in October, beating the same horse by a greater distance over 2m 4f.

Upped in trip to an extended 3m for a novices' chase when last seen at Cheltenham's Showcase meeting in October – a race the yard won with Chicago Grey prior to his victory here – he beat the in-form 144-rated Soldier Of Love by seven lengths, staying on strongly after hitting the front two from home despite making a few jumping errors along the way.

This extended break has always been the plan, and it's something former trainer, Gordon Elliott, executed to perfection with Tiger Roll who came here having also not run since October. Galvin also has strong Festival form having finished a solid sixth in the 2019 Ballymore Novices' Hurdle to go with his second-placed effort over fences 12 months ago.

A strong travelling sort, he'll likely be held up off the pace before creeping his way into contention on the final circuit. Good ground would aid his cause.

The McNeill Family-owned **Escaria Ten** looks sure to thrive over this marathon.

The son of Maresca Sorrento has been the subject of plenty of support in recent weeks after keeping on well without threatening Eklat De Rire in a Grade 3 at Naas over 3m 1f on his latest start. Before that he was an impressive winner of a 3m beginners' chase at Thurles in December, jumping well and effortlessly coming clear to record a wide-margin success over Ministerforsport.

Despite being a seven-year-old, he's a huge individual and still likely to be developing both mentally and physically which leads me to believe we are only just scratching the surface in terms of his ability. He's very much a horse on an upward trajectory and remains completely unexposed in these staying races. He does, though, have the option of running in the Ultima Handicap Chase – a race which his owners sponsor.

Pencilfulloflead's form ties in closely with a few of these having beaten Coko Beach by three parts of a length on chase debut at Galway back in October and then trounced Latest Exhibition by seven lengths in a Grade 2 at Punchestown the following month, both races over an extended 2m 6f.

Stepped up to Grade 1 company for the Faugheen Novice Chase at Limerick on Boxing Day, he perhaps found the extended 2m 3f too sharp and was pipped in the dying strides by Colreevy who was in receipt of 7lb. He then conceded weight to the field when stepped up to 3m 1f in a Grade 3 at Naas where he finished third behind Eklat De Rire and Escaria Ten, keeping on well at the one pace having jumped a little novicey.

A dour stayer, he would relish the ground if it came up soft but his jumping needs to improve if he's to have a say in the finish.

Paul Nolan went close to winning this race in 2019 with Discorama and looks to have an outstanding chance two years on with **Latest Exhibition**.

The Grade 1-winning hurdler finished a neck behind Monkfish in last year's Albert Bartlett Novices' Hurdle and has suffered defeat at the hands of the same horse on his last two starts over fences: firstly, by three lengths over 3m at Leopardstown's Christmas meeting and then by 11 lengths in a first-time tongue-tie over an extended 2m 5f at the Dublin Racing Festival when last seen. On both occasions he moved through the race strongly and displayed a resolute attitude before being outclassed in the closing stages.

He did, though, make a winning chase debut at Punchestown back in October, beating School Boy Hours by two lengths over an extended 2m 6f before finishing seven lengths adrift of Pencilfulloflead over the same course and distance.

Thoroughly likeable and sure to stay, he would come under serious consideration if he ran here, although his trainer has spoken of skipping Cheltenham altogether in favour of the Irish Grand National.

Willie Mullins' strong stayer, **Lord Royal**, makes plenty of appeal despite lacking in experience.

Having taken a crunching fall when still travelling well at the penultimate fence on chase debut at Thurles back in November, he then ran well below par over an inadequate trip of 2m 3f at Naas the following month before returning to something like his best at Navan when stepped back up to 3m, staying on well but failing by three parts of a length behind Mr Hendricks.

That form now reads well with the third, The Big Dog, winning the Punchestown Grand National Trial and Lord Royal looks to be coming to the boil at the right time. If he gets into a rhythm with his jumping, he's sure to come home well.

Martin Brassil's **Longhouse Poet** has a touch of quality and accounted for Monkfish in a bumper at the Punchestown Festival in May 2019 before placing at Grade 1 level over hurdles, firstly behind Envoi Allen at Naas in January 2020 before getting within two and a quarter lengths of Latest Exhibition the following month at the Dublin Racing Festival.

Success over fences came at the fourth time of asking when upped in trip to 3m 1f at Punchestown on New Year's Eve, making most of the running and seeing his race out strongly despite a sloppy leap over the last to beat Run Wild Fred by one and a half lengths with the same distance back to The Big Dog in third.

That's good form with the runner-up filling the same spot in the Thyestes Chase from a mark of 136 on his next start, whilst the third won on a revisit to Punchestown in February from a mark of 136 and his run before that ties him in with Lord Royal.

Longhouse Poet is a dark horse over fences, reflected in his handicap rating of 142 as opposed to his mark of 145 over hurdles. He adds further substance to a race already not lacking in quality.

The home team is headed by **Royale Pagaille** who has come of age this season, winning all three starts impressively, including twice in handicap company from marks of 140 and 156, resulting in his rating rising to 166 which more than entitles him to a crack at the Gold Cup.

An uncomplicated sort of horse, he travels powerfully through a race and his clean, quick jumping can be a real asset. He has, though, appeared completely at home on testing conditions, something he may not be guaranteed on the opening day.

Paul Nicholls could run Soldier Of Love and Next Destination.

Next Destination, officially rated on a mark of 153, has won a pair of Grade 2 chases this season, the latter over 3m at Warwick where he beat Fiddlerontheroof by one and a half lengths, jumping well and going away at the finish. Prior to that he won the John Francome Novices' Chase over an extended 2m 7f at Newbury, again jumping well and never stronger than at the line.

Experienced at the Festival having finished fourth, beaten three lengths, by Fayonagh in the 2017 Champion Bumper. He also finished third to Samcro in the Ballymore Novices' Hurdle the following year before beating Delta Work by a neck in a Grade 1 over hurdles at the Punchestown Festival.

Seriously smart on his day, he would be one they all have to fear if he came here.

Soldier Of Love pulled up when last seen. That was on soft ground at this course in a race won by The Big Breakaway. Prior to that he chased home Galvin, also at this course, having won three times on the trot over 3m 2f at Newton Abbot. Good ground suits him well but he has a little to prove.

David Pipe is having a good season and his recent Grade 2 Reynoldstown Novices' Chase winner, **Remastered**, commands respect. He stayed on well that day, beating the 142-rated course and distance winner, Demachine, by four lengths having produced a spring-heeled round of jumping from the front.

That success followed on from victories at Carlisle over 2m 4f in November and a comfortable win over 3m at Wetherby in December, on both occasions making all and relishing the fences.

A rating of 146 suggests he won't be far away, but with all his success coming on ground soft or heavy, he may be taken out of his comfort zone on quicker conditions. He is, though, a very good jumper, which counts for a lot.

Ben Pauling knows what it takes to win this race having saddled Le Breuil to success in 2019 and he looks to have a lively outsider two years on with **Nestor Park**.

Connections have always rated the eight-year-old and he appears to have turned a corner this season with the application of cheekpieces, running to a good level of form and finishing second in a competitive handicap chase behind Morning Vicar over 2m 4f at Newbury in November. He then finished fifth behind Clan Legend at Aintree the following month over the same distance, jumping well bar a peck on landing over the open ditch (eleventh), causing him to lose his pitch before plugging on up the straight, shaping like a horse in need of further.

With the step up in trip to 3m 2f came improvement as he was narrowly beaten by Amateur on a revisit to Newbury and then once again filled the runners-up spot, this time behind Lieutenant Rocco at Ffos Las over 3m, jumping low over a number of his fences and losing his position before plugging on again down the straight.

On official ratings he has over a stone to find with a few of these, but he's a consistent sort of horse and a relatively safe jumper. He's also likely to improve for the greater stamina test. He's a fun each-way sort of bet at 50/1.

Charlie Longsdon's tough race mare, **Snow Leopardess**, needs respecting if she runs here.

The Grade 2-winning hurdler made a good start to her chase career at Bangor in September, finishing third to The Butcher Said over 3m before chasing home the subsequent Grade 1 winner Shan Blue at Wetherby. Off the mark in game style at Haydock over an extended 3m 1f in November when staying on strongly to defeat Commodore by a half-length, she then went down by three-quarters of a length in the Grade 3 Rowland Meyrick on Boxing Day, battling all the way to the line before being touched off by Canelo.

Colin Tizzard's **Sizing At Midnight** was pulled up on unsuitably heavy ground when last seen but he has some good form on better conditions, winning over 3m 2f at Newton Abbot back in August and then again over 3m at Ffos Las in October before finishing a good second to Kitty's Light at Exeter later that month. He also would have gone close in the Badger Beers Silver Trophy at Wincanton had he not fallen three from home.

His stable companion, **Ofalltheginjoints**, has winning form over 3m and acts on a variety of ground but probably isn't good enough to trouble some of these.

Happygolucky is a good jumper with strong course form. He is also rated not too far behind some of these and could go well at a price, although this distance may test his stamina to the limit and the Ultima is likely to be the more favoured option.

Eden Du Houx has failed to build on the promise he showed in bumpers and others make more appeal despite him being unexposed over this sort of trip.

Golan Fortune is worthy of his place and is a strong stayer over three miles but is unlikely to be good enough here, whilst **Acey Milan** can be an unreliable jumper and is better suited to soft ground.

Of the others worthy of mentions, Kerry Lee's **Demachine** is a progressive young chaser but is held by Remastered. **Port Of Mars** beat **Milanford** by 10 lengths over 3m 1f at Hereford in January but was pulled up last time whilst **Salty Boys** has shaped like a thorough stayer but probably isn't quite up to this level.

Nick Gifford's **The Mighty Don** could go well at a price. He comes into his own when the emphasis is on stamina and will appreciate the return to better ground.

Welsh National winner, **Secret Reprieve**, is unlikely to come here whilst **Dickie Diver** is running out of time to qualify. If he did manage to sneak in, you couldn't rule him out with any degree of certainty.

James Nash's **Forza Milan** is a good yardstick in these staying chases but was a well-beaten fourth here 12 months ago and is held on various lines of form. That comment also applies to **Eurobot**, although he is still young and also lightly raced. He may not have reached his peak.

Conclusion

Galvin is a warm favourite and has been for some time, but this has the feel of an above average renewal with the likes of Latest Exhibition bringing genuine Grade 1 form to the table. Then there's Pencilfulloflead, Next Destination and Remastered, all Grade 2 winners over fences whilst Royale Pagaille has produced form this season entitling him to a crack at the Gold Cup. Of those, Next Destination is a horse I have the utmost respect for.

However, I'm taking a chance on Escaria Ten as I believe his form will rise to a new level over this sort of trip. The same can be said for the unexposed Lord Royal, whilst I'll also be looking to Nestor Park to outrun his odds of 50/1. (Jodie)

Escaria Ten (Lord Royal, Next Destination, Nestor Park)

Day Two

Look at the top of the ratings – ten of the last 12 winners were either top or second-top rated. Recent winning form also offers a clue – 20 of the last 26 winners won last time out. A good race for horses aged five or six accounting for 27 of the last 28 winners.

A few of those at the top of the market are more likely to run elsewhere.

Appreciate It, Metier, Ballyadam, Dreal Deal and Blue Lord are probably heading for the Supreme, while Bear Ghylls is also in the Coral Cup.

Gaillard Du Mesnil became favourite for this after beating 12 rivals in a Grade 1 contest over 2m 6f at Leopardstown last month. Held up in sixth on the inside, he lobbed along jumping well before making progress into second approaching the turn for home. Gently nudged along he joined stable companion Stattler and went clear to win by five lengths from Gentlemansgame, who took second close home.

Before this the winner had beaten Mr Incredible over 2m 4f without coming off the bridle, having run second on his hurdling debut at Punchestown in November.

When trained in France he won once and ran second four times in AQPS bumpers over trips up to an extended 1m 6f, including two runner-up places in Graded company.

This son of Saint Des Saints does not lack speed. He travels very smoothly through a race and can quicken at the finish. It could be argued that he didn't beat anything of note last time, but the second, third and fourth in his previous race all won next time out.

Willie Mullins will have a line to the form of second favourite **Bob Olinger** through Blue Lord, who ran second to Henry de Bromhead's six-year-old in the Grade 1 Lawlor's Of Naas Novice Hurdle in January.

The son of Sholokhov won a point-to-point before easily winning a bumper at Gowran Park last March, making all to win by 10 lengths. He gave Ferny Hollow a race when running him to a length on his hurdling debut back at Gowran in November before making all to land odds of 1/8 at Navan in December.

His three runs over hurdles have been on soft/heavy and heavy ground but his trainer thinks he will be suited to better ground.

Bob Olinger is not quite as fluent a hurdler as the favourite but he possibly has the superior form. They are hard to split.

Bravemansgame brings useful form into the race, having beaten the 147-rated Star Gate by 10 lengths in the Grade 1 Challow Novices' Hurdle, with The Glancing Queen back in third.

Before that he won novice hurdles at Exeter and Newbury, racing prominently on each occasion.

The six-year-old can be a little hesitant at the occasional hurdle but he goes a strong gallop and handles good ground. He has had wind surgery but there has been no sign of weakness in his finish.

I rate his form superior to that shown by the two Irish contenders, but I'm not convinced his hurdling will be as fluent in the hurly-burly of this big field.

It's only a marginal issue, but of the three Gaillard Du Mesnil possibly has the best turn of foot.

Looking elsewhere the unbeaten **Bear Ghylls** will have his supporters. You can't have his record without being useful at least, and the form he showed to give 6lb to Gowel Road at Ffos Las reads especially well, but he doesn't settle in his races and is not a natural jumper. Even his trainer Nicky Martin says his jumping is "appalling".

The stronger pace may suit him here at Cheltenham and he is bred to stay the trip, but he appears to have learnt nothing in his three runs and his sloppy jumping may cost him dearly.

Cape Gentleman, who pulled up behind Gaillard Du Mesnil at Leopardstown, returned to winning ways in the 2m Dovecote Novices' Hurdle at Kempton. He won over 2m 4f on his hurdling debut at Punchestown but this will be tough for him.

The favourite's stable companion **Stattler** is more likely to run in the Albert Bartlett. The four-year-old **Duffle Coat** is very tough but reported unlikely to be at the meeting. If he does run, then the Supreme looks the more obvious option. **Make Me A Believer** could outrun his odds if he turns up here.

N'golo is better than he has looked in his last two starts, but he has a number of other options. Dan Skelton seems reluctant to run **Wilde About Oscar** at the meeting. **Adrimel** may also bypass the meeting.

Benson is expected to improve for the step up in trip given the way he powered home last time in a handicap at Ascot. He had won his previous three starts and would be the best outsider were this his chosen target.

Conclusion

It must be long odds against this race going to a horse outside the top three in the betting.

They are hard to fault, as they each stay well and seem to be progressive. Bob Olinger and Bravemansgame look more galloping types than Gaillard Du Mesnil, who had the pace to run consistently well in AQPS races over middle distances in France.

The way this race is likely to be run should allow his rider the chance to settle him in the pack and deliver his challenge approaching the last.

In what promises to be a decent race I marginally favour Gaillard Du Mesnil. (Marten)

Gaillard Du Mesnil (Bob Olinger)

The Brown Advisory Novices' Steeple Chase (Grade 1)
3m abt ½f

1.55

A good race for horses aged seven – they have won 15 of the last 20 renewals. Not a good race for French-bred horses – no wins despite being represented 35 times over the last 14 years.

"What I particularly liked at Cheltenham was that when they got tight down to the last and after the last, he put his head down and went through it. He's maturing and the penny is starting to drop. You need a horse that understands racing. That's what Hurricane Fly and Quevega did; they understood the point to win. I'm not sure Monkfish knew that at the very start but now he does."

Those were the comments of Patrick Mullins on **Monkfish** right at the beginning of the season. If the Susannah Ricci-owned seven-year-old didn't understand racing last year, he still made a right good job of it, and it's hard to contradict Mullins's depiction now, with the gelding three from three over fences, including two brilliant Grade 1 performances at Leopardstown.

Reportedly, a big raw horse when he first landed in Closutton, Monkfish only just made the Punchestown Festival for his seasonal debut in a bumper, in which he finished second and the following season he was beaten on his first start over hurdles by Noel Meade's Diol Ker.

Since then he is unbeaten and has done nothing but progress. A 20-length win in a usually informative W.T. O'Grady Memorial Novice Hurdle at Thurles set him up for an Albert Bartlett bid and he showed guts and tenacity to fight off both Fury Road and Latest Exhibition late on in that contest.

So far over fences he hasn't needed to show guts and tenacity because he's just been too good – faultless in a beginners' chase win at Fairyhouse before always holding his old rival Latest Exhibition in the three-mile Grade 1 Neville Hotels Novice Chase at Leopardstown over Christmas.

Meeting that rival again, this time over two miles and five furlongs in the Flogas Novice Chase, Monkfish was even more impressive, jumping his fences like hurdles and ridden supremely confidently by Paul Townend, and he eased away from Latest Exhibition again after the last, without being asked with any force. The time of that contest was all of six seconds faster than the time the 140-rated Off You Go ran in the Leopardstown Handicap Chase later on the card, which solidified the impression Monkfish made. Indeed after the race, Willie Mullins reported that the first thing Paul Townend had said to him was that he should be in the next race (that being the Irish Gold Cup).

Monkfish is a dual Grade 1-winning chaser whose ceiling hasn't been found yet – he has just three starts over fences and eight starts on the track in all – and he has the Festival form already in the book. He looks rock solid.

The same owners, Susannah and Rich Ricci, have the Venetia Williams-trained **Royale Pagaille** as an option for this race, after the third season novice progressed sharply through the handicap chase ranks this season, winning all three of his races and progressing to a mark of 166. At this stage, it seems more likely he will go for the Gold Cup because the Riccis have Monkfish and because he has accumulated the necessary experience to make him a suitable contender for that race, despite his novice status.

Latest Exhibition is a less doubtful runner but may well switch to another target as his trainer Paul Nolan is fed up of bumping into Monkfish (scoreline is currently 3-0 to the Mullins runner). If he did line up, he deserves respect. He got much closer to Monkfish over three miles at Christmas than he did over two miles and five furlongs in the Flogas. However it's too simplistic to suggest that he will get closer to Monkfish again back at three miles, for all that good ground and the longer distance appear to suit him better.

Eklat De Rire is another Irish-trained horse prominent in the betting. Henry de Bromhead's seven-year-old is two from two over fences, opening his account in a beginners chase at Punchestown before improving to take a Grade 3 contest over three miles and one furlong at Naas.

He jumped and travelled well in that contest, eventually seeing off the challenge of Escaria Ten after the last but it should be pointed out that he got the run of things from the front and both he and the runner-up were receiving 8lbs from **Pencilfulloflead** in third.

That former Gordon Elliott-trained runner had earlier shown good form to beat Latest Exhibition and finish second to Colreevy in the Grade 1 Matchbook Betting Exchange Novice Chase, but was probably below that sort of form at Naas.

To these eyes, Monkfish's main opposition comes from Britain, firstly with **The Big Breakaway**. Colin Tizzard's gelding has always been well thought of and was sent off as short as 8/1 in Envoi Allen's Ballymore Novices' Hurdle last season, coming off the back of two impressive performances. He got outpaced coming down the hill before running on to take fourth in that contest but nonetheless, it was still a promising run by the former winning pointer who changed hands for €360,000. With the second half of that sentence in mind, it was always going to be fences for him this season and he made a good start when winning his novice chase by 10 lengths at Cheltenham.

He was turned over at long odds-on by Bold Plan when going back in trip at Exeter, but he had to make his own running there and probably got found out when the pace of the race quickened up late on. There was an element of that in his performance to finish second in the Kauto Star Novices' Chase too. Having not looked 100% comfortable travelling on that flat course, he still looked like he was coming to claim Shan Blue in the straight only to be outjumped by the Dan Skelton horse who had come into that race on the crest of a wave and mostly had his own way in front.

There were elements of the same trainer's Native River's performance in the same race a few years ago and for me The Big Breakaway will be much better suited to a more stamina-laden three-mile trip and also should benefit from a generally more positive outlook from the runners in his yard, a team who for large parts of this season, including at Christmas, have looked out of sorts.

Sporting John has to be a player as well. Another Irish point winner, he had a similar sort of hurdles profile to The Big Breakaway, only he dealt with the pace of last year's Ballymore more poorly, trailing in 30 lengths behind the winner after failing to find any sort of rhythm from an early stage.

His chasing career got off to a terrible start when, having travelled and jumped well enough in a beginners chase at Exeter, he failed to finish off his race at all, eventually trailing in 33 lengths away from Fiddlerontheroof. Something was clearly amiss there and he was given plenty of time before being thrown right back into the deep end in the Grade 1 Scilly Isles Novices' Chase at Sandown. It looked ominous for him early on in that contest when he made a bad mistake at the fifth that shuffled him to the rear of the field, but he managed to work his way back into the race for Richard Johnson and eventually did what The Big Breakaway failed to do, reeling in Shan Blue with a sustained effort up the Sandown straight.

The pace was strong in that race and you could see he benefited from that aspect from his positioning, but it's to devalue his performance when you consider it was just his second start over fences and he had the class to get himself back into a Grade 1 race and ended up beating a Grade 1 winner, the pair of them clear. He still lacks experience but the move to three miles could unlock further improvement and he shouldn't be written off.

Next Destination was third to Samcro in the 2018 Ballymore before landing a Grade 1 over three miles for Willie Mullins at the Punchestown Festival. He reportedly suffered a host of injury setbacks prior to making his return to the racetrack, in the hands of Paul Nicholls, in the Grade 2 bet365 Hurdle at Wetherby at the beginning of this season. He finished a good second to the classy mare Roksana there before being sent straight over fences and straight into the deep end in the usually informative Grade 2 novice chase at Newbury's Ladbrokes Winter Festival.

Before that race (just short of three miles), he had reportedly schooled well and was well backed, and he jumped and travelled accordingly, seeing off a couple of useful but limited sorts in One For The Team and Kalooki. Next Destination's only other run came in the Hampton Court Novices' Chase at Warwick, a somewhat tactical three-runner contest in which he showed good tactical speed to grab the initiative from Fiddlerontheroof, with Golan Fortune, fourth in the Kauto Star, further back.

The son of Dubai Destination has run well at two Cheltenham Festivals (finished fourth in Fayonagh's Champion Bumper) and clearly retains the ability he showed over hurdles. However his lack of experience and the form of his two wins suggest he has a bit to do to make a real impact, and he looks short in the market with that in mind.

In contrast, **Fiddlerontheroof** has plenty of experience over fences and though he was beaten by Next Destination at Warwick, his third second in a row and fourth in all this season, the nature of that tactical contest may not have suited him. His previous three seconds had all come over shorter distances but he still ran well behind good horses – notably If The Cap Fits first time out at Ffos Las and the talented Allart at Ascot.

His run in the Hampton Novices' Chase at Warwick was his first start over three miles and the Tizzards firmly believe that the further he goes the better he'll be. That's an interesting observation given he has only had one start at three miles and that race in itself didn't look like a truly run contest. His three defeats have all come at short prices which may lead to plenty potentially underrating him now up in class.

Secret Reprieve is interesting given he is a novice winner of a Welsh National but he was 8lbs well in at Chepstow and, even after that win, is rated at 144. He'd likely be better off in handicap company and Aintree could be his overall target. **Longhouse Poet** is another who will probably end up elsewhere but the form of his previous win at Punchestown really catches the eye. On his first start over three miles plus, he did well to outstay both Run Wild Fred and The Big Dog, who have substantially upgraded that form with big handicap chase performances on each of their subsequent starts. It's likely that a mid-140s mark would tempt connections to go for a handicap chase instead.

Finally, **Remastered**, another with options elsewhere, should not be discounted after he made it three wins from three runs in the Reynoldstown at Ascot, outstaying the strong-travelling and previous course-and-distance winner Demachine. He has done most of his racing on soft or heavy ground, so those sorts of conditions could well be important to him. He needs to improve from his overall form but improving is what he is doing and he showed a very good attitude at Ascot in a race that often throws up a good quality staying chaser – O'Faolain's Boy used it as a platform to success in this contest, for so long known as the RSA Chase, in 2014.

Conclusion

Unoriginal, but Monkfish looks head and shoulders above all the staying novice chasers so far this year and with his proven ability to act around Cheltenham in the heat of a Festival battle, it's really hard to see past him. If odds-on shots aren't your thing, take a chance on either or both of the Colin Tizzard-trained pair – The Big Breakaway and Fiddlerontheroof. Both give the impression a testing three-mile chase will bring about their best and they could be underrated on account of the stable's form earlier this season. (Ronan)

Monkfish (The Big Breakaway)

The Betway Queen Mother Champion Steeple Chase (Grade 1)
Abt 2m
3.05

Festival winning form is a good indicator – 12 of the last 20 winners were previous Festival winners. Recent winning form is also important – 16 of the last 22 winners won last time out. Look at horses aged seven or over – only three of the last 46 winners were aged six or younger.

The highlight on the second day, the Queen Mother Champion Chase, has seen many riveting and emotional encounters. It will be no different this time, with many willing Altior to record his third success in the race. Whether he can do so is very much in the balance, with the bookmakers' ante-post price of 7/1 or thereabouts suggesting he has deteriorated to a degree.

The red-hot favourite as things stand is **Chacun Pour Soi**, a nine-year-old bidding to give Willie Mullins his first victory in the race. A horse with a fascinating background, he spent 1,089 days on the sidelines dating from his final run at Enghien for Emmanuel Clayeux to his first for Mullins at Naas, a modest affair where his reputation preceded him and he started at 4/9 and won well.

Since then his record has been all but impeccable – six more races with five more wins, four of them at Grade 1 level. He is clearly a horse out of the very top drawer but there have been two more extended absences of 239 and 309 days. It would appear that Mullins has to monitor him very closely indeed.

Having said that, he has had three outings this season, winning the Grade 2 Kerry Group Hilly Way Chase at Cork, the Grade 1 Paddy's Rewards Club Chase at Leopardstown and the Grade 1 Ladbrokes Dublin Chase at the same course. He won easily at odds-on each time, Mullins having also chosen the last two of those races the previous season, when his one defeat came after a lengthy absence and A Plus Tard proved just too strong in the Paddy's Rewards race.

An outstanding steeplechaser, Chacun Pour Soi is unquestionably the one to beat at Cheltenham and the only worry concerns his long spells on the easy list. He is a very short price indeed for a horse that must have worried connections at some stage. Then again, Mullins is the outright master of his trade and everything has gone well of late.

Nicky Henderson's **Altior**, one of the very best two-mile chasers of the modern era, won his first eleven races over obstacles and eight more after his first wind operation. Those victories included the Champion Chase in 2018 and 2019, the first of them at a remarkably generous even money when Henderson was worried a setback might leave him short. Only fifth running down the hill, he rallied bravely and forged clear in the closing stages, almost bringing the house down in the process.

He needed a longish break after a second wind operation and found Cyrname too good in the three-runner Grade 2 Christy 1965 Chase at Ascot in November 2019. That was over 2m 5f, in line with Henderson's belief that a longer trip was overdue, but Altior reverted to two miles for the Grade 2 Game Spirit Chase at Newbury in February 2020. He won, none too impressively, at 1/3 but had the better part of a year off afterwards and found Nube Negra too strong in the Grade 2 Desert Orchid Chase at Kempton last December. Rising 11 and with two operations behind him, he was probably starting to feel the strain.

Nube Negra, from the thriving Dan Skelton stable, had previously been beaten seven lengths by Rouge Vif in the Grade 2 Agetur UK Kingmakers Novices' Chase at Warwick, form which leaves him with something to find, though he is younger than the two market principals. He also finished second to Esprit Du Large in the Henry VIII Novices' Chase at Sandown – a race flattered on this occasion by its Grade 1 status.

A Plus Tard has raced three times since accounting for Chacun Pour Soi at Leopardstown. He was a little disappointing when favourite and only third in the Grade 1 Ryanair Chase at Cheltenham and was then absent until Navan in November, where he started at 2/1 on but could not quite handle Castlegrace Paddy in the Grade 2 Tote Fortria Chase.

That was over two miles but he stepped up to three for the Grade 1 Savills Chase at Leopardstown over Christmas and found remarkable reserves on the run-in to get up and beat the redoubtable Kemboy and Melon in a driving finish. It is impossible to equate what he achieved there with the challenge of a Queen Mother Champion Chase but Henry de Bromhead knows what it takes to win this race and A Plus Tard warrants respect.

Politologue, a credit to Paul Nicholls, finished second to Altior in 2019, beaten just under two lengths. He went one better last year when given a very positive ride by Harry Skelton and had the race won by the time they reached the last.

There were major disappointments in a five-runner race, most notably the favourite Defi Du Seuil, well held at 2/5, while **Sceau Royal** was never involved at all. That takes nothing away from Politologue, who has tried much longer trips in his time and won the Grade 1 Melling Chase at Aintree over two and a half miles in 2018 and finished fourth in the King George at Kempton later the same year. He is reliable and always gives of his best, winning the Betfair Tingle Creek Chase at Sandown last December before finding Kim Bailey's **First Flow** on a real 'going' day in the Grade 1 Matchbook Betting Exchange Clarence House Chase at Ascot in January. There seemed no fluke about it as First Flow pulled seven lengths clear.

The going was soft that day (and for Politologue's previous six races), which helped First Flow as well, though he is even more effective on heavy. He was winning his sixth race in a row and 14/1 was a generous price, the general feeling being that he wanted it like a bog, not merely soft.

His three bloodless wins in lesser company early in 2020 were all on heavy and, in a most unusual 18-race career, he has raced on soft or heavy 17 times and only once on good to soft!

Bailey has aimed him at soft targets in all respects but form is form and there was nothing soft about beating Politologue quite easily, a performance which should not be underestimated. In the unlikely event that it comes up soft or softer in mid-March, he would undoubtedly be a key player.

Trying to second guess Mullins' moves is a rash exercise, but **Melon** surely needs further these days while **Min** won the Grade 1 Ryanair Chase over the extended two and a half miles last year and was pulled up on his only outing since then over a shorter trip. The trainer has various options for both of them, while Henderson will almost certainly let the enigmatic **Buveur D'Air** try for a third Champion Hurdle.

On the other hand, Alan King's Sceau Royal would presumably run a great deal better than last year and looked close to his best when recently accounting for Champ, who needed further, in the Grade 2 Betfair Game Spirit Chase at Newbury. On that running he would have nothing to fear from the free-running **Greaneteen**.

Preferred to these is De Bromhead's consistent mare **Put The Kettle On**, who won the Grade 1 Arkle last year and again showed her liking for Cheltenham when taking the four-runner Grade 2 Shloer Chase last November. True, she was well held in third when Chacun Pour Soi won the Grade 1 Paddy's Rewards Club Chase at Leopardstown not so long ago, but she makes each-way appeal and looks a natural over two miles. She has won six of her eight races over fences and, in a race where there are question marks over one or two, she looks solid.

Fakir D'oudairies was a good second to Put The Kettle On in the Arkle. He is only six and there may be more to come. The layers are not keen on the form line or may believe there are alternative races for the pair, hence the big prices, but Arkle form has often been franked in the Champion Chase in the past.

Conclusion

Although Chacun Pour Soi has had problems over the years, he has a wonderful Grade 1 record and the last three races, all wins, came regularly enough. There is no logical reason to oppose him despite lingering doubts about the value.

Altior may have gone back a little more than people realise, brilliant though he has been in the past. The suggested dangers, if they line up, are the pair from last year's Arkle, Put The Kettle On and Fakir D'oudairies. The position would change in the event of heavy ground (highly unlikely), which would suit the underrated First Flow. (Ian)

Chacun Pour Soi

The Glenfarclas Cross Country Steeple Chase
3m 6f

3.40

Course experience helps here – 13 of the last 16 winners had run at the course previously. Not a great race for Willie Mullins or Paul Nicholls – no winners from a combination of 25 runners.

Having taken home a total of 13 trophies from a possible 16 since the race's inauguration in 2006, this has been a happy hunting ground for the Irish, especially trainer Enda Bolger who is responsible for five of those victories with the likes of Spot Thedifference and Garde Champetre who later became household names in this sphere. More recently it's been Gordon Elliott stealing the show, firstly in 2017 with Cause Of Causes and then twice with Tiger Roll in 2018 and 2019, which he famously followed with victories in the Grand National at Aintree.

Last year we saw a changing of the guard with the French-trained six-year-old **Easysland** spoiling the party, dethroning Tiger Roll to the tune of 17 lengths and recording a first success for France and indeed his trainer, David Cottin.

The son of Gentlewave arrived here 12 months ago in the form of his life having won five times on the bounce, including twice around the cross country fences at Pau and Compiegne before recording a seven-length beating of his stable companion, Amazing Comedy, over this course and distance in December 2019, surviving one serious blunder before making the best of his way home from the fifth last under Jonathan Plouganou.

After another victory back at Pau in February 2020 when donning the colours of J P McManus, all roads led to the Festival where he was a warm order, going off at odds of 3/1 behind race favourite Tiger Roll at 8/11.

Never too far from the pace, his jockey rode a clever ride, switching from left to right and right to left, hugging the inside line and saving ground the whole way. Easysland jumped well, only making a semblance of a mistake over the timber rails (eighth) before moving to the lead at the 20th fence. From there he looked in control and had enough petrol left in the tank to widen the gap between himself and the second on the climb to the line.

Preparations this time haven't been so straightforward, as he comes here after only one run which was a surprise beating over course and distance at Cheltenham's November meeting where he lumped around plenty of weight and made a couple of momentum-costing mistakes late on.

Cottin could also be represented by **Disco D'Authie**. At 12 years of age, he is certainly in his twilight years and was well beaten by Easysland at Pau last February over an extended 3m 7f. He also looks to need testing ground.

Tiger Roll requires no introduction but may need to produce a career best if he's to have his place in history by winning this race for the third time.

On official ratings, the pint-sized 11-year-old is still 1lb ahead of Easysland on a mark of 168, but after finishing sixth of nine in a 1m 6f maiden on the Flat at Navan in October, he's been pulled up over course and distance here in November and finished last of six, 65 lengths behind Beacon Edge, in the Grade 2 Boyne Hurdle at Navan when last seen in February – a race he won in 2019 before claiming glory here.

Exceptionally talented – a bit of a freak in truth – it's incredibly hard to rule out a return to form, especially as he comes alive here, recording four Festival victories including a Triumph, a National

Hunt Chase and two Cross Countrys. You do have to wonder, though, if the years and indeed the miles are catching up with him.

Christian Williams' 2019 Welsh National winner, **Potters Corner**, shaped with more than a touch of promise on his first spin over course and distance in November when third behind Kingswell Theatre.

Held up in rear and unhurried over the fences by Jack Tudor, the 11-year-old jumped carefully in the main but was a little clumsy over the banks, the cheese wedges and the water on the second circuit. From there he steadily picked off the opposition, moving into fourth over the Aintree fence before staying on strongly up the hill.

Forced to miss his chance to build on that effort at the December meeting due to a dirty scope, he has since run twice over hurdles, finishing seventh of 13 at Warwick in January before pulling up on bottomless heavy ground at Exeter. Those efforts do not inspire confidence but his trainer hopes that run was just a blip and a recent schooling session over these fences went to plan with Williams stating he's never seen his horse look or school better.

Guaranteed to stay and open to improvement in this discipline, he'll certainly be an interesting each-way angle against the short-priced favourite.

Enda Bolger's new kid on the block, **Shady Operator**, is worth more than a look after returning the comfortable winner of the P.P. Hogan Memorial Cross Country Chase over the banks at Punchestown in February.

That was the eight-year-old's first go in this discipline, but he had clearly been well schooled at home, jumping professionally throughout under a confident ride from Derek O'Connor who produced him to lead between the final two obstacles before staying on strongly to the line.

Although lacking in experience over this course, I'm sure he'll acclimatise quickly and even if this is not his year, he's likely to be a name we'll hear plenty more of in the future. Better ground is likely to suit.

Third behind Shady Operator at Punchestown was **Space Cadet**.

He kept on well without being a match for the front two but with winning form over an extended 3m 4f, he'll likely be better suited to this trip. A good run can be expected provided he takes to the fences.

Some Neck is interesting.

Fairly useful in his days with Willie Mullins, the ten-year-old has raced three times for John McConnell, only beating two home in a Grade 2 hurdle at Navan in November before finishing a promising third behind Neverushacon in the Risk Of Thunder Chase over the banks at Punchestown later that month, responding well to his jockey's urgings having been pushed along before the fourth from home.

He then built on that effort over this course and distance in December, taking to the fences like a natural and only making slight errors over the railed hedges (tenth and eleventh). Tracking the pace, he lobbed along in his comfort zone and responded willingly for his jockey from the bottom of the hill, clawing back the four-length deficit with the leader from the final fence to get up on the line.

Officially rated on a mark of 137, he's a fair way behind those at the head of the market, but he has a touch of class and I can see him running a good race.

Second and fifth to Some Neck at Cheltenham were Defi Des Carres and Beau Du Brizais.

That was **Defi Des Carres'** first start for Charlie Mann having gained plenty of experience over cross country fences in his native France, including a race in Compiegne where he finished seven and a half lengths adrift of Easysland in October 2019 before going on to win over 3m 2f on heavy ground at Lyon Parilly the following month.

Pulled up when last seen over regulation fences at Plumpton, he arrives here with something to prove. He did, though, enjoy himself over these fences and will probably run well without being good enough.

Beau Du Brizais ran a very good second to course specialist, Kingswell Theatre, here in November but couldn't land a blow on his revisit to the track despite plugging on at the one pace up the straight. He's taken to the fences well but needs to produce a career best if he's to reverse that form.

Further behind Some Neck in December was **Kingswell Theatre**. He loves it round here, as he demonstrated when bounding to victory in November, but this is his fourth go at the Festival and, so far, he's struggled off level weights.

Kings Temptation was no match for Kingswell Theatre when sixth to him in November. He has since run OK in a jumpers' bumper hinting at a return to form, but winning here is a far stretch of the imagination. **Vivas** also finished in behind Kingswell Theatre and has since been pulled up in the race won by Some Neck. He loves good ground but hasn't shown anything to suggest he's good enough to win here.

Diesel D'Allier hasn't won since claiming victory over this course and distance in November 2019 and was well beaten into fourth at the Festival last year. **Out Sam** finished third 12 months ago but could only manage fourth behind Some Neck in December. He was ridden quietly that day but at 12 years of age, his best days look to be behind him.

Henry de Bromhead's **Balko Des Flos** was rated on a mark of 169 in his pomp and demonstrated he still retained some of his old ability when running seventh to The Storyteller in a Grade 1 at Down Royal in October. Although untried in this discipline, his class could carry him a long way.

Saint Xavier always shapes like a horse capable of more than he shows. He was pulled up last time in the Edinburgh National but ran well in a first-time visor at Kempton the time before. There's nothing to suggest he'll go close here, but he'll crop up somewhere, one day.

Hogan's Height and **Lord Du Mesnil**, like a few others here, look to be using this as a stepping stone to the Grand National. The latter would love the ground if it came up heavy. **Le Breuil** is a good jumper and could run well if he takes to this new discipline. **Alpha Des Obeaux** has been pulled up on his last two starts but he's rated on a mark of 145 which is higher than many of these.

Veteran and prolific point-to-pointer, **Kruzhlinin**, is more likely to run in the hunters' chase on Friday.

Conclusion

Given Tiger Roll and Easysland both have something to prove, this could be the time to take them on and I'll be looking to Some Neck to go well at a decent price. There was much to like about Potters Corner's debut over this course and distance and he'll be plugging on at the finish, although with the Grand National his main objective, Christian Williams may have left something to work on. Shady Operator could be the dark horse for Enda Bolger. (Jodie)

Some Neck (EW)

**The Weatherbys Champion Bumper
(A Standard Open NH Flat Race) (Grade 1)
2m abt ½f**

4.50

A good race for raiders from the Emerald Isle – Willie Mullins has trained ten winners plus 21 of the last 28 winners were trained in Ireland. Recent form is imperative – the last 17 winners won last time out.

With a phenomenal record reading ten victories from the last 18 renewals and the 1-2 in last year's contest for good measure with Ferny Hollow beating the race favourite, Appreciate It, Willie Mullins is the obvious place to start as he once again looks to have the race by the scruff of the neck.

Starting with **Kilcruit**, the six-year-old created a visual impression incomparable with probably anything else we've seen this season, across any discipline, when romping to success in the Grade 2 Goffs Future Stars Bumper at Leopardstown's Dublin Racing Festival.

Anchored towards the rear under Patrick Mullins, he travelled powerfully behind the strong pace before gradually moving closer over half a mile from home. Without so much as a squeeze from the saddle, he was quickly on the premises before picking off the leaders with the minimal amount of fuss and breezing up the run-in to record an emphatic 12-length success over Letsbeclearaboutit with a further nine lengths back to his stable companion and previous winner, Whatdeawant.

Whether the race fell apart around Kilcruit, making the performance appear more impressive than it was, is open to debate, but the fractions would certainly back up that theory. However, he won in a similar fashion on stable debut at Navan back in December, albeit against inferior opposition.

With Kilcruit you have an uncomplicated horse who travels powerfully through a race. He also has tactical pace to deal with any trouble in running together with the stamina to come home up the hill.

Willie Mullins' stranglehold on this race tightened when the news broke that he would now train **Sir Gerhard** after Cheveley Park – who are bidding to win this race for the third successive time – removed all their horses from the care of Gordon Elliott.

Purchased for £400,000 having been an impressive 12-length winner of a point-to-point for Ellmarie Holden in November 2019, the gelding wasted no time in demonstrating his talents under Rules scorching home at Down Royal in late October, beating The Banger Doyle by an impressive 14 lengths.

That success was followed by a Listed bumper at Navan in December – a race previously won by Envoi Allen and Samcro – where he handled the testing conditions and powered clear inside the final furlong to cross the line with four and a half lengths to spare over Letsbeclearaboutit.

Uncomplicated and blessed with both a high cruising speed and the ability to quicken, the tactics are going to be fascinating between these two market leaders. Of the two, Sir Gerhard is probably blessed with the greater speed.

The Closutton trainer also has a strong back-up team.

Ramillies has small claims but having been an impressive 10-length winner at Leopardstown over Christmas, he was no match for Kilcruit last time. He possibly paid the price for being too close to the pace and kicking too early, but it's hard to envisage him reversing that form.

Cool Jet was fairly well supported on his debut in a strongly contested bumper at Leopardstown on Boxing Day but could only manage fourth place behind Harry Alonzo. He followed that with an easy victory at Thurles in February, travelling strongly throughout and ploughing clear in the heavy ground inside the final furlong to beat one of the outsiders by five lengths. He looked good on that occasion and has a pedigree which suggests we may see even more improvement on good ground.

The following three all receive a useful 7lb fillies' and mares' allowance.

For whatever reason **Grangee** failed to fire in a Listed mares' bumper at Market Rasen when third to Eileendover but produced a career best in the Grade 2 mares' bumper at the Dublin Racing Festival, staying on from the rear to beat Party Central by a neck with a further four and three-quarter lengths back to her stable companion and race favourite, Brandy Love.

Brooklynn Glory was unbeaten in two starts prior to finishing fourth, beaten just shy of eight lengths, by Grangee at Leopardstown. She may have struggled with the testing underfoot conditions that day as her trainer stated after her debut victory that she might want better ground.

Take Tea was further behind Grangee in that Leopardstown bumper, weakening between the final two furlongs having taken a keen hold in the early stages. She looked very smart on her debut at Naas but now has a bit to prove.

Three Stripe Life lacks vital experience but on the little evidence to hand looks a high-class prospect.

The five-year-old son of Leading Light created a lasting impression at Navan in late January when sluicing through heavy ground to come clear in very taking fashion to beat Outlaw Peter – who now enters training with Paul Nicholls – by nine lengths. It wasn't so much the winning distance that was impressive but the manner with which the gelding dispatched his rival once given the signal passing the furlong pole, instantly injecting pace having travelled powerfully throughout.

With just the one start, it raises the question of whether he'll be ready for this step up in grade but he is certainly a talent to be reckoned with. I like him a lot.

Hollow Games' form ties in with Sir Gerhard having also beaten The Banger Doyle, albeit by the shorter distance of seven lengths, on his debut at Punchestown (The Banger Doyle also finished last of ten in the Grade 2 won by Kilcruit), stretching clear and easing in the closing stages. He then followed up under a penalty at Leopardstown but shaped like more of a stayer than a horse with gears, staying on strongly for pressure to beat the subsequent 19-length maiden hurdle winner, Eurotiep, by just shy of two lengths.

Visually not as impressive as some but undoubtedly talented. He will appreciate an end-to-end gallop and will not shirk a battle.

Eyewitness was given a good ride by Jamie Codd to get off the mark at Naas in February having finished third there on his debut the previous month. I liked the way he knuckled down and stretched right to the line, but this is much tougher. He is, though, related to some smart horses on the Flat and that pace could take him a long way if he came here.

Dan Skelton's **Elle Est Belle** is another who will benefit from the 7lb mares' allowance and has been trained specially for the race.

The daughter of the late Fame And Glory quickened clear to win in a hack canter on her debut at Aintree back in October and looked for all money the winner of a Listed mares' contest at Cheltenham the following month only for the result to be called a dead heat with Ishkhara Lady sharing the spoils.

With the yard in flying form all season and with all-important course form, it's hard to rule out a bold show although victory would be a surprise.

Paul Nicholls has a few lovely young horses in Gold Bullion, Shearer and Rainyday Woman which he can call upon.

We haven't seen **Gold Bullion** since he made a winning racecourse debut at Warwick in January where he beat a seven-runner field by upwards of four and a half lengths. He was a little green that day and the lack of experience is a worry for him here.

Shearer produced a strong staying performance to win by nine lengths at Warwick on New Year's Eve and looks a horse very much on the improve. Whether he has quite enough tactical pace for this race remains to be seen but the team like him very much and he could run into a place.

Rainyday Woman by contrast has plenty of experience to call upon having had two spins for Pam Sly last season before joining current connections at the start of this term for whom she remains unbeaten. She's a six-year-old and receives the 7lb mares' allowance and could go well at a price. She's a strong stayer and won't be fazed by the hill.

Gavin Cromwell's **Letsbeclearaboutit** looked a useful type when bolting up in a pair of bumpers at Tipperary and Punchestown in the early part of the season but was no match for Sir Gerhard when upped to Listed level at Navan and was beaten four and a half lengths at the line. He then filled the same spot 12 lengths behind Kilcruit at the Dublin Racing Festival, setting a strong pace throughout before giving way two furlongs from home.

The Richard Spencer-trained **Wonderwall** made a winning debut at Ascot in November and returned to that track the following month to finish third in a Listed contest. He stuck on well that day, chasing home two from Paul Nicholls' yard, but that level falls some way short of what's required here.

Harry Whittington's **Brave Kingdom** made a good impression when getting off the mark at the first time of asking under Rules at Fontwell but in winning he beat a horse who had previously finished 10 lengths behind the aforementioned Wonderwall. Although entitled to improvement, he'll find life much tougher here.

Arthur's Seat is just one of a handful of horses Paul & Clare Rooney kept when they cut back their numbers under National Hunt rules and despite him being a four-year-old he's fairly experienced. Twice a winner from four starts, he stayed on strongly last time at Kelso but he shouldn't be good enough to have a say here.

Ben Pauling's **Fine Casting** got off the mark at the third time of asking when beating Mumbo Jumbo by a length and a half at Newbury on heavy ground in January, making all and keeping on well despite running green. Prior to that he finished second to Might I, and that horse's form ties in with **I Like To Move It** having finished in behind him when they met in the Listed bumper at Newbury. A line through that form says Nigel Twiston-Davies' gelding has the measure of Fine Casting, but neither look Champion Bumper class, although I Like To Move It will appreciate the greater stamina test.

Twiston-Davies could also field the dual bumper winner, **Super Six**. He's a big strapping horse who gallops forever. He'll make a lovely chaser down the line but may be taken off his feet in the early stages here.

Of the others to mention, **Creggan White Hare** got off the mark at the fourth time of asking when scoring by a head at Newcastle. **Chemical Energy** will need to raise his game considerably to close the 21-length deficit with Kilcruit whilst **Jack's A Legend** has been beaten twice at this course.

Last term, **Eric Bloodaxe** beat Ferny Hollow on racecourse debut at Fairyhouse before getting the better of Wide Receiver at Leopardstown. No match for Appreciate It on a revisit to that track for a Grade 2 bumper, it's a huge ask for him to be at the top of his game after over a year away from action.

Laura Morgan's yard is flying, and her **Dom Perry** created a good impression when winning at Fakenham last month. He stayed on in good style there and was well on top at the line, but this is a much tougher task.

Pressure Sensitive came clear in good style to win under a penalty at Wetherby in February having scored by a neck on his debut back in October. **Socks Off** won an all-weather bumper and makes up the numbers.

Conclusion

It's hard to get away from the two at the head of the market here with tactics likely to play a huge part in the result. If the ground came up good, Sir Gerhard's natural pace and turn of foot could enable him to get away off the home bend, although Kilcruit's stamina will kick in when he hits the hill. You do have to wonder, though, if the change of yard plays a part in a horse's mental well-being before a big day and for that reason, I side with Kilcruit whose preparations have being uninterrupted.

Of the rest, I respect Three Stripe Life and also Rainyday Woman if she came here. (Jodie)

Kilcruit (Three Stripe Life, Rainyday Woman)

Day Three

Look for horses who were successful in a Graded novice chase last time out – all ten winners of this race contested one while nine of the ten winners finished first or second. Older horses should be avoided as only one winner was older than seven.

Another Grade 1 novices' chase, another odds-on favourite, another Festival win for Envoi Allen?

For many it should be that simple but Cheveley Park's decision to move their horses out of Gordon Elliott's yard last week, following the emergence of a shocking picture of the trainer sitting upon a dead horse, is a curveball in this market that absolutely no one saw coming.

The seven-year-old was only ridden out for the first time at Henry de Bromhead's gallops on Wednesday 3 March which gives him less than two weeks at his new base when you take into account travel time over to the course. Exactly what the disturbances or difficulties that will present to him are unknown but Paul Nicholls has suggested that the change of yard is far from ideal preparation. I have no idea what the difficulties will be but a new environment, new feed, new hay, new bedding and new people/rider is surely going to have some sort of effect.

It makes Envoi Allen, for all that his raw ability surely will cover a large part of this equation, a difficult odds-on proposition to analyse. But let's start with what he has achieved this year.

He began his season at Down Royal where he jumped brilliantly and won easily from January Jets, a subsequent winner. He then built on that to land the Grade 1 Drinmore Novice Chase at Fairyhouse, again jumping perfectly and wasn't extended to score by more than eight lengths from Assemble. He looked set to be tested significantly when meeting Asterion Forlonge at Punchestown but that runner's unseat at the first made things easier for him and again, he didn't blow anyone away but jumped beautifully and won as he liked.

If you're taking him on, you're likely to point to his chase form, not yet nearly as strong as what he achieved over hurdles last term, and in all, he has beaten just 11 rivals. On the flip side, his wins have come a lot more easily – his jumping perhaps affording him that luxury – and a feature of all three of his races has been the confidence Jack Kennedy has displayed on him, most notably on his latest start at Punchestown where the runner-up Fils D'oudairies got very close to him at one stage in the straight, before he cleared away with what appeared to be the minimum amount of fuss.

It was also notable that Kennedy reported that he blew hard after his Drinmore win and Gordon Elliott confirmed after the race that he hadn't worked the horse hard, and that Cheltenham was the number one plan. This was Elliott's number one horse and the Marsh had been the number one target all season – you can be sure that up until last week, his preparation had been meticulously planned.

He is readily proven at Cheltenham with two Festival wins already and in truth, unlike the Arkle, there doesn't seem to be a meaningful level of competition to him. It's over to you, Henry.

Since the Envoi Allen news, there have been small semblances of money for Energumene, who won his beginners chase over this distance but has been seen to much better effect over two miles. Presumably that money was the result of the possibility that Envoi Allen may not run but it's probably unlikely that Willie Mullins will reroute him here. The same applies to Monkfish, whose target most of this season has been the Brown Advisory Novice Chase.

However this has long been the target of **Shan Blue** as he was given no other option even in the initial entries for all three novice races.

Dan Skelton's seven-year-old failed to make an impact when stepped up in class after his maiden hurdle win last season, but he has improved significantly for chasing and is another whose jumping is a joy to behold. He began his career with a smooth novice chase win at Wetherby, over just short of two and a half miles, but marked himself out as a potential Grade 1 novice when conceding 13lbs to classy mare Snow Leopardess in a 16-length win in another novice chase at Wetherby, this time over three miles. That form looked even better when the runner-up won a valuable contest at Haydock and finished second to Canelo in the Rowland Meyrick back at Wetherby.

On the same day as the latter, Shan Blue confirmed his Grade 1 potential by landing the Kauto Star Novices' Chase from the well-hyped The Big Breakaway. Again his jumping was key and on this occasion probably the difference between victory and defeat because having led for much of that three-mile contest, he looked a sitting duck to the Colin Tizzard horse in the straight but managed to hold on to his lead through accurate jumping.

Since that contest, Skelton seems to have concluded that two and a half miles is his trip, alluding that his jumping was the making of him and he would be better served over a distance where that attribute was more significant. He suffered his first defeat at the hands of Sporting John in the Grade 1 Scilly Isles at Sandown, but for many he still emerged as the best horse in that contest. Leading most of the way, he saw off the persistent challenges of Messire Des Obeaux and Paint The Dream only to give way to Sporting John, who had been well off the pace early on.

That Philip Hobbs-trained runner is a talented sort on his day but appeared to have benefited from the pace of the contest, Shan Blue and the others going hard up front, and the sectionals prove this – a reported 93% closing speed of the front two tells the story. It was to Shan Blue's credit that he got as close as he did and for me he looks like the biggest threat to Envoi Allen and one who has rock-solid place claims in the Marsh.

As a winner of a Grade 1 over two and a half miles, **Sporting John** would be a logical contender for this race but is a more likely candidate for the Brown Advisory Chase over three miles, given his owner is likely to have Chantry House to run here (more or less confirmed by his trainer Nicky Henderson last week) and given the way he stayed on at Sandown.

With **Chantry House**, it's still all potential rather than real substance. He looked good in two novice hurdles over two miles last season before connections hummed and hawed over running in the Supreme or Ballymore, opting for the former in which he stayed on nicely for third behind Shishkin and Abacadabras.

That gave rise to the prospect that he could be a real Marsh contender this season but, as of yet, he hasn't really convinced. He posted a 26-length win on his chase debut over two miles at Ascot but beat just two other runners there, before disappointing behind Fusil Raffles when given his first chance over two and a half miles in a novice chase at Cheltenham in December. The testing surface was given as an excuse for his disappointing effort and while he looked smooth when travelling and jumping well to beat Coconut Splash, to whom he conceded 6lbs, at Wetherby on his latest start, that form still looks a level below the standard expected here.

For instance, the runner-up had finished second to Messire Des Obeaux on his previous start and that horse was well held in the Scilly Isles.

Allart, Hitman and **Dame De Compagnie** all looked like legitimate strong contenders for this race before falling/unseating on each of their previous starts and now it seems their trainers favour other options.

Chatham Street Lad has other options as well but would be a fascinating contender if showing up here. A nine-year-old novice chaser who won off a mark of 118 at Ballinrobe in October, the Mick Winters-trained gelding doesn't have the profile of a Grade 1 novice chaser, but his form, and the time of one of his wins in particular, doesn't lie and he would be a threat to Envoi Allen, especially on a soft surface.

He has progressed rapidly over fences this season, and his five-length defeat of Off You Go, subsequent winner at the Dublin Racing Festival, in a two-mile handicap chase at Cork reads even better now but he smashed his career best again with a 15-length win in the Caspian Caviar Gold Cup, seemingly prospering by switching off for his rider when racing behind a solid pace. He finished that race all of 6.2 seconds faster than Fusil Raffles, a likely rival in this race, earlier on the card, which proves it was no fluke.

He was beaten in the usually very competitive Dan & Joan Moore Memorial Handicap Chase at Fairyhouse, over two miles, but that run wasn't a disgrace at all. Clearly the return to the course and distance of his Caspian Caviar romp is key, although connections could also be tempted by the Paddy Power Plate, run over the same distance, with the big field for that contest more likely to mirror the Caspian Caviar Gold Cup scenario he prospered in.

Fusil Raffles was heralded as one of the stars of the season by his trainer Nicky Henderson in a press Zoom call the other week and while that appraisal is somewhat superfluous, the Grade 1-winning juvenile hurdler has gone a little under the radar this term, given he has three wins from four runs, two of which have come at Cheltenham.

It's not that long since the six-year-old went off 2/1 favourite for the Christmas Hurdle and though he didn't develop into the Champion Hurdle horse connections had hoped for last season, he has developed promise again as a novice chaser.

His first two wins came over two miles but he disappointed when favourite for the Grade 2 novice chase at Cheltenham's November meeting, with the soft going there given as an excuse for him pulling up. Upped to just over two and a half miles on the new course in December, he produced a real stern staying performance to beat Lieutenant Rocco and stablemate Chantry House. He was third turning into the straight that day but reeled in the former-mentioned rival in a slow-motion finish which suggested that he could go even further again. Despite him winning on soft ground there, Henderson reiterated his preference for a faster surface.

His overall form and times suggest he has plenty to do but his previous class as a hurdler and Cheltenham know-how should be taken into account.

The mare **Colreevy** is worth noting. She is three from three over fences and a Grade 1 winner after she outstayed Pencilfulloflead admirably in the Matchbook Betting Exchange Novice Chase at Limerick over Christmas. That is good form, especially defeating that runner on a heavy surface, and she looked as good as ever back against her own sex at Thurles, recording a facile 12-length win. In a normal year, that is a year without Envoi Allen, it would probably make sense to go for this race and receive weight off the geld ings rather than go for the Mares' Chase and concede weight to her own sex because of that Grade 1 penalty.

Latest Exhibition would be another fascinating contender. Second on each of his previous three starts, the latest two to the high-class Monkfish at Grade 1 level, his trainer Paul Nolan came out with interesting reflections after his latest defeat at the Dublin Racing Festival. The Wexford trainer has naturally become frustrated with finishing second to Monkfish (losing 3-0 in that personal head-to-head battle) and was seeking other options for his stable star. This race would be one of those options (along with the National Hunt Chase) and though Nolan bemoaned the fact that he'd have to face Envoi Allen here, the bare fact that it's not Monkfish he'd be facing again could yet entice him.

If he did turn up, he would have to be one of Envoi Allen's main rivals, and in truth, he looks as effective if not more at this intermediate distance than he does at three miles, especially when you take into account his hurdles form as well (Grade 2 winner over two and a half miles and found only Abacadabras too good in Grade 3 over two miles).

The likely decent surface at Cheltenham will suit him and he has proven himself at the track, given his excellent effort to finish third in the Albert Bartlett last season. There has been no news on his target since Nolan's comments but you can back him at 16/1 non-runner no bet with plenty of firms and that looks more than fair. If he showed up, he'd be half that price at least.

Conclusion

Let's hope Envoi Allen, one of the star names of National Hunt racing, shows up here without any complications and can give his best running. He was the pick for this race prior to last week's news but with his preparation getting messed up, from a betting point of view, he looks worth taking on at odds-on now. I believe Latest Exhibition would have a big say in this race but it seems like connections are keen to swerve the meeting. That leaves Shan Blue, whose brilliant jumping will be a huge asset at Cheltenham. Chatham Street Lad, if returning to the scene of his Caspian Caviar Gold Cup win, should not be underestimated either. (Ronan)

Shan Blue (Chatham Street Lad)

The Ryanair Steeple Chase (Grade 1) 2m abt 5f — 2.30

Look at the top of the market for pointers – 14 of the last 16 winners featured in the top three in the betting. Proven winning distance is important – the last 13 winners had won over a minimum of 2m 4f.

The Ryanair has one of the most open markets in the build-up to the 2021 Festival with most layers going at least 5/1 the field. It is a tricky contest to evaluate, especially with Willie Mullins having a handful of possible contenders including both Min and Melon. Perhaps surprisingly, they just give best in some lists to stable companion Allaho, who may not have fulfilled his potential to date but almost certainly has more to offer.

Allaho owes his position in the market to two performances. He was a very good third to Champ and Minella Indo in the Grade 1 RSA Insurance Novices' Chase at the big meeting last year and recently battled on well to hold stable companion Elimay in the Grade 2 Horse & Jockey Hotel Chase at Thurles.

In the Cheltenham contest he hit the 12th and was again far from fluent three out but still had every chance on the run-in, going down by a length and the same. Horses involved in a tight finish at Cheltenham invariably reproduce their form there and Allaho fits the bill. His form this season is not as impressive because he was never a factor in the Grade 1 John Durkan Memorial at Punchestown, a race won by Min, and then finished a well-beaten fourth behind A Plus Tard, Kemboy and Melon in the Grade 1 Savills Chase at Leopardstown.

That was a hotly contested race, of course, and it was only in the closing stages that he dropped away. He clearly stays three miles well, as the RSA showed, but dropping back to 2m 5f will not be a problem on Thurles evidence. Improvement is required, however.

Imperial Aura, who represents the in-form Kim Bailey, is another with significant Cheltenham experience, having won the Northern Trust Company Novices' Handicap Chase at the Festival last year. Bailey has the happy knack of picking up races around the smaller tracks and Imperial Aura started this season with victory (at 7/4 favourite) in the Colin Parker Memorial Intermediate Chase at Carlisle. Moving on to Ascot, he won the Grade 2 Chanelle Pharma 1965 Chase, beating Itchy Feet by five lengths at 13/8, and started at even-money for the four-runner Grade 2 Ladbrokes Silviniaco Conti Chase at Kempton, only to unseat David Bass at the second. That was uncharacteristic and a great pity because the race would have told us plenty about him. Master Tommytucker won it with Clondaw Castle, a very good winner of a hot handicap at Kempton the other day, in second. Imperial Aura is very consistent indeed and has risen from 143 to 163 in the ratings. He would have started favourite for the Paddy Power Gold Cup at Cheltenham in November but Bailey felt the race came soon enough and gave him more time. He is a convincing candidate in the Ryanair and that Kempton mishap is the only time he has failed to complete.

Min, who won the Ryanair twelve months ago, is a marvellous old character (if ten can be called old, though he seems to have been around a long time) with plenty of Cheltenham experience to his name, including a fifth in the Champion Chase at one stage. Successful in ten of his 18 chases, he led some way out for Paul Townend last year and just repelled Saint Calvados by a neck with A Plus Tard and Frodon next.

Resuming in style this season, he won the Grade 1 John Durkan Memorial at Punchestown by a length from Tornado Flyer with Melon over six lengths away in third. The only 'blot' came next time when he made a serious mistake at the seventh and had to be pulled up in the Grade 1 Ladbrokes Dublin Chase at Leopardstown, won by the very impressive Chacun Pour Soi. If fully over the experience Min may go close again but he has been to the well many times in his career.

Although Chacun Pour Soi looked different class, **Fakir D'oudairies** fared best of the rest and, although his form is mixed, a similar effort would carry him close in this.

Saint Calvados has not truly come on for last year's second – his fifth race in a row at Cheltenham. Off for several months, he finished a fair fourth in the Grade 1 King George VI Chase at Kempton (won by Frodon at 20/1) but unseated Gavin Sheehan at the 17th when already being niggled along in the rerouted Grade 2 Virgin Bet Cotswold Chase at Sandown, won by Native River. That was over three miles on heavy ground and if trainer Harry Whittington is thinking along those lines at present, 2m 5f on a faster surface this month may not be ideal.

Frodon is a willing character who goes very well for Bryony Frost, especially when allowed to bowl along in front. He won the Matchbook Betting Exchange Handicap (3m 1f) at Cheltenham in October but was headed some way out in the Grade 2 William Hill Many Clouds Chase (fences omitted) at Aintree in December and could finish only fourth of five. That made his King George triumph something of a surprise but he was out and clear while others struggled to go the pace in a messy race. Well held in the Ryanair last year, Frodon has raced over three miles plus since then. Much will depend on whether he is allowed to dominate, if indeed this ends up being his target.

Frodon and **Kemboy** both figure at around 10/1 for the Ryanair and both are quoted at 14/1 for the Gold Cup. Kemboy, an admirable battler on home turf, has shown a marked dislike for the Cheltenham showpiece in the past and it is hard to see him matching strides over this shorter trip.

Melon has something to find with Min on John Durkan form last December but has since finished third behind A Plus Tard and

Kemboy in a gruelling Savills Chase at Leopardstown. That may have left its mark because he finished last of five behind Kemboy in the Grade 1 Paddy Power Gold Cup.

He does have form at shorter trips and went under by inches to **Samcro** in the Grade 1 Marsh Novices' Chase at the Festival last year. Samcro has not shone in two outings this season, finishing third of five behind Battleoverdoyen in a Grade 2 chase at Down Royal and then pulling up in the Savills Chase.

Considering the options available to him, Nicky Henderson seems to have left the Ryanair to **Mister Fisher**, who likes Cheltenham and jumped particularly well when outpointing Kalashnikov in the rerouted Grade 2 Fitzdares Club Loves The Peterborough Chase in December. Clondaw Castle was a few lengths away in third but has since won a very valuable handicap. Four of Mister Fisher's last five outings have come at Cheltenham, including when pulled up this season in the Paddy Power – lost a shoe, ground too soft but only 11/2 in a very competitive race – after winning the Ryman Novices' Chase last term and finishing fourth in the Grade 1 Marsh Novices' Chase. Strictly speaking he has ground to make up on Samcro and Melon but almost certainly has more scope.

Conclusion

Willie Mullins wins so many top-class NH races that it is hard to criticise the odds on offer about any of his horses. Even so, Allaho does seem rather short on what he has achieved of late.

Despite the claims of Min, Melon and Fakir D'oudairies it is possible to imagine the prize staying at home this year and the advice is to cover both Imperial Aura and Mister Fisher. It is great to see Kim Bailey back with Cheltenham chances and Imperial Aura has gone from strength to strength, the one blemish coming when he unseated David Bass at Kempton. Mister Fisher has a fine record at Cheltenham and has scope for further improvement.

Interestingly, Imperial Aura would probably have started favourite for the Paddy Power in November and Mister Fisher very nearly did at 11/2. One didn't make the party and the other was pulled up after losing a shoe and disliking ground softer than the official description. Perhaps one of them will make up for lost time. (Ian)

Mister Fisher (Imperial Aura)

The Paddy Power Stayers' Hurdle (Grade 1) abt 3m

3.05

Look at horses who contested the Cleeve Hurdle on their previous start – this accounts for eight of the last 14 winners here. Avoid older horses as only one of the last 48 winners was older than nine.

The Stayers' Hurdle brings together some old and familiar faces and has been notable over the years for horses which return again and again and become firm favourites – Baracouda, Inglis Drever and Big Buck's being three good examples.

Paisley Park has not reached that level but will carry plenty of sentimental support, having won the race two years ago and faltered through no fault of his own last time. This season he has looked more than capable of regaining his crown at the age of nine. Thyme Hill is closely tied in with him on form, while there are interesting challengers with good handicap performances to their name who may step up. The market is more open-looking than in some of the other Grade 1 races.

Paisley Park, trained by Emma Lavelle, first started to attract serious attention in the 2018/19 season when he left behind a poor effort in the Albert Bartlett Novices' Hurdle the previous spring with five straight victories out of five.

Starting off in handicaps, including a very valuable one at Haydock, he graduated to Grade 1 company and won the Long Walk Hurdle at Ascot, closing to lead after the last and beating West Approach by two lengths. That looked an ordinary renewal of the Long Walk (West Approach started at 40/1) but Paisley Park went on to Cheltenham and squashed any suggestion that the course might not suit him by surging between horses to take the Grade 1 galliardhomes.com Cleeve Hurdle in fine style.

He attracted support down to favouritism that day and was soon market leader for the Sun Racing Stayers' Hurdle itself, starting at 11/8. Once again he travelled well, hit a minor 'flat' spot on the turn for home but then quickened up and led at the last, pulling away to beat Sam Spinner and former champion hurdler Faugheen by just under three lengths and four. It became obvious that Aidan

Coleman is the perfect jockey for him and allows for the brief spell when Paisley Park needs to be bustled along.

Now the likely favourite for any long-distance hurdle he contested, Paisley Park started well the following autumn, winning the Grade 2 Ladbrokes Long Distance Hurdle at Newbury by a hard-earned length from the determined Thistlecrack. He repeated his success in the Cleeve at 4/6, beating Summerville Boy by just over a length without impressing everyone, then started at the same price in the Stayers' Hurdle, Paddy Power having taken over sponsorship.

On the face of it he was very disappointing. There was no recovery when he hit his habitual flat spot and running to the last he was clearly under strong pressure. He found little on the run-in and dropped away to finish seventh behind shock 50/1 winner Lisnagar Oscar. He lost his left-fore and right-hind shoes in the race and a heart condition was later diagnosed.

The latter explanation met with understandable sympathy, especially for owner Andrew Gemmell, who was born blind and is a wonderful supporter of racing. Paisley Park seemed to recover and returned to work with a heart monitor fitted. All seemed well because he returned at Newbury for the Long Distance Hurdle and kept on well for second behind Philip Hobbs' Thyme Hill, to whom he was conceding 3lb.

The form worked out perfectly in the Grade 1 Porsche Long Walk Hurdle at Ascot because Paisley Park engaged in a protracted duel with Thyme Hill and beat him by a neck at levels in heavy ground. This, surely, indicated that he was over his problems and would take the beating in the Stayers', even if there was precious little to spare over his old rival.

Thyme Hill is consistent, handles good and heavy ground and his chance is obvious from the above. At seven he is two years younger than Paisley Park and his Cheltenham record is very good indeed. Third in the Weatherbys Champion Bumper in 2019, he won the Grade 2 Ballymore Novices' Hurdle in November of that year and finished fourth in the Albert Bartlett twelve months ago. He is understandably second favourite as things stand and looks a major threat.

A point should be made about the horses finishing third in the latest two races mentioned above. Paul Nicholls' **Mcfabulous**, favourite at Newbury, seemed not to stay three miles and has been dropped back in trip, disappointing at Fontwell on his latest outing, while Dan Skelton's consistent mare **Roksana**, third in the Long Walk at Ascot, was well held by Paisley Park and Thyme Hill on the run-in. Even with the mares' allowance she could not quite bridge the gap, which is a major factor in the decision (not yet cast in stone) to go for the Mares' Hurdle. She is covered in that section.

Sire Du Berlais is a fascinating contender and clearly deserves his place in the line-up after winning the Pertemps Network Final at the Festival for the last two years. Owned by JP McManus, he landed quite a gamble at 4/1 favourite in 2019, beating Tobefair by a neck, and followed up last year at 10/1 off a 7lb higher mark, just outpointing stable companion The Storyteller, who was receiving 3lb. He likes Cheltenham, having also finished fourth in the Martin Pipe Conditional Jockeys Handicap Hurdle in 2018.

It may be best to view Cheltenham as far and away the most important target where Sire Du Berlais is concerned. He started the current campaign with a victory in the Grade 2 Lismullen Hurdle at Navan but then managed only third behind Flooring Porter and The Storyteller in the Grade 1 Leopardstown Christmas Hurdle. He was never quite in contention there and finished just behind The Storyteller, which is at odds with the way they came home at Cheltenham last March.

Sire Du Berlais is capable of beating **The Storyteller** at level weights, having conceded 3lb in the second of his Pertemps triumphs. He has been rested since Leopardstown with the Stayers' Hurdle in mind, whereas The Storyteller possibly surprised connections with a very good second (at 20/1) to Kemboy in the Grade 1 Paddy Power Irish Gold Cup, again at Leopardstown. The bookmakers respect Sire Du Berlais at around 8/1 for the Stayers but The Storyteller, with other possible targets, has recently been available at 20/1.

Flooring Porter, trained by Gavin Cromwell, is even bigger. This is strange, given the way he dominated the Leopardstown Christmas Hurdle, where the distances were six lengths and three-parts of a length. He started at 11/1, having been rated 136 when winning a good handicap by a dozen lengths at Navan the time before. He was raised a stone for that and has gone up another 10lb after Leopardstown, putting him within 5lb of Paisley Park and 2lb superior to Sire Du Berlais. At this point the 'Cheltenham factor' enters the equation, of course, and in quoting Flooring Porter at 25/1 the layers fully expect the JP McManus horse to turn the tables one way or another.

Lisnagar Oscar is probably regarded as a fortunate winner of the Stayers' last year, given the way Paisley Park dropped out. He was on a losing run of seven when landing the big race at 50/1 and had started at that price when only third behind Paisley Park in the Cleeve. This season has not gone well and he finished only seventh of 10 behind Thyme Hill and Paisley Park in the Grade 2 Ladbrokes Long Distance Hurdle at Newbury, after which he underwent wind surgery. A recent second to Third Wind in the Grade 2 Rendlesham Hurdle at Haydock was a step in the right direction but there is a long way to go.

The likes of **Champ** and **Kemboy** would be making an unlikely return to hurdles but the Gigginstown pair **Beacon Edge** and **Fury Road** (held by Sire Du Berlais) could go well at big prices after fighting out the finish to the Grade 2 Boyne Hurdle at Navan.

Conclusion

However well Paisley Park performs after his heart problem, he has hardly anything to spare over Thyme Hill and there is still the worry about his tendency to tread water at the crucial moment. He will need to be right back to his 2019 best to win this.

Lisnagar Oscar does not have the form to follow up but The Storyteller and Fury Road are both capable of making an impression. However, course specialist Sire Du Berlais has almost certainly been brought along with this race in mind and is the main recommendation.

Flooring Porter is way overpriced on Leopardstown running but this will be a very different game at a much faster pace. (Ian)

Sire Du Berlais

The Parnell Properties Mares' Novices' Hurdle (Grade 2)
2m 1f

4.15

The Willie Mullins race – all five winners were trained by the trainer and all five began their career in France. By contrast, Nicky Henderson has no wins despite eight entries over the years.

Much the way he has dominated the Mares' Hurdle since its introduction, Willie Mullins has farmed the Mares' Novices' Hurdle with a perfect five-from-five record since the race was introduced to the Festival.

The Irish champion trainer has long been a big supporter of the improving programme for mares, and for a long time he has put his money where his mouth is, never afraid to direct some of his big owners' investment into mares. It's no wonder he is a huge advocate for mares' races at the Festival – you reap what you sow.

It is not a surprise that Mullins has the favourite for this year's renewal, albeit a marginal one, and it's probably fair to say he doesn't have a Limini or Laurina type this term. He does however have a Let's Dance type because **Hook Up** shares a very similar profile to that 2017 winner.

Like her, Hook Up is owned by Susannah Ricci, is a second season novice having run in the Triumph Hurdle last season, and returns to the Festival now an improved mare and one who can this time take on her own sex.

Unlike Let's Dance, she was disappointing in the Triumph, where she failed to make any sort of impact, and she hasn't been able to get on a winning streak like that mare did but she has definitely improved and showed as much first time out when 12 lengths too good for Gars De Sceaux in a Fairyhouse maiden hurdle.

She returned to that Meath track for a mares' novice hurdle just after Christmas and was well backed to make it two out of two there, only to be well and truly put in her place by Royal Kahala, who quickened past her easily after she was awkward at the last. That was a case of 'back to the drawing board' but I thought it was interesting that she was allowed to run in the Grade 1 Chanelle Pharma Novice Hurdle at the Dublin Racing Festival instead of going for the likely easier option of the Paddy Mullins Mares' Handicap Hurdle.

She was a 50/1 shot against Appreciate It there but she really caught the eye with her run to finish fourth. Her jumping was a little sketchy, with the result that she was a little far back than ideal turning into the straight, but she really picked up well from there and having looked likely to be well held, she stayed on nicely to finish just seven and a half lengths away from the winner.

That is strong form in the context of the Mares' Novices' Hurdle, this year's renewal especially. Her jumping is a concern and she has to make up plenty of ground on Royal Kahala, but that latest effort at Leopardstown suggests she has taken a step forward. And, it goes without saying, she is in the hands of a trainer who knows how to prepare a mare for this contest.

Royal Kahala has taken the Honeysuckle novice route, doing almost all of her racing at Fairyhouse. Peter Fahey's mare has been brought along patiently and having finished fifth in a Punchestown bumper in October, she improved to win a mares' bumper at the Meath track in November before returning to the course ten days later to take a mares' maiden hurdle, where she had the useful The Getaway Star well held in second.

She stepped up markedly on that when too good for Hook Up in early January. There, she always travelled well but got caught for room between the last two flights. She had to be switched and was a length or two off the Mullins mare coming to the last, but was able to take advantage of her rival's mistake, though she probably would have won anyway given the way she finished her race off on the bridle.

Sent off 11/10 favourite for the Grade 3 Solerina Mares Novice Hurdle (often an excellent guide and won recently by Honeysuckle, Limini and Laurina), she found only Roseys Hollow too good, but lost very little in defeat, given she was conceding 4lbs to that older mare and she still finished in front of Gauloise and Mighty Blue, who had earlier in the season fought out the finish of a Listed mares' hurdle at Thurles, and the front four were clear.

She'll likely meet Roseys Hollow again here, but on 9lbs better terms, which is significant. On all form lines, she probably deserves to be a marginal favourite.

Roseys Hollow has only had four runs over hurdles but has taken a significant leap forward on each of them, and could well do so again. She is trained by Cork-based Jonathan Sweeney and began her season with a decent fourth to Delvino in a mares' maiden hurdle at Naas. She then beat Global Equity comfortably at Fairyhouse, with that runner boosting the form since by finishing second in higher-class races.

Roseys Hollow impressed in the Solerina, jumping and travelling really well for one so inexperienced and though Royal Kahala came hard at her, she never looked like relinquishing her lead after the last. You could only be positive about her after that but with regard to this race, she'll have to carry a penalty because of her win, and in all, faces a 9lb weight swing with Royal Kahala, and though less significant, 3lbs with Gauloise. She could well improve again to do that but both those mares, and others, have similarly unexposed profiles, and could step forward again as well.

Gauloise could easily step forward and deserves automatic respect given her trainer and also her owner, Kenny Alexander, who has targeted buying top-class mares with great success.

She beat Global Equity, a mare who links plenty of form lines in Ireland this year, comfortably at Thurles on her Irish debut before returning to that Tipperary track to smoothly win a Listed novice hurdle in December from **Mighty Blue**, the pair of them clear. Both those mares went on to finish third and fourth respectively in the Solerina, so that does present a solid look to the form. Gauloise will need to improve but she has plenty of scope to do so and shapes as if a stiff two miles will suit.

The shortest-priced British-trained runner is Alan King's **The Glancing Queen** who has run in the last two Champion Bumpers (finished seven-length fifth and then 23-length eighth) and won the Grade 2 mares' bumper at Aintree in between.

Given what she showed in bumpers and that she has had plenty of time, connections could well be disappointed with a two from four record over hurdles this season, with her two wins coming at odds-on in mares' novice hurdles. That said she was a good third to Bravemansgame in the Grade 1 Challow Hurdle, form which may not be too dissimilar a level that Hook Up ran to behind Appreciate It.

She came back in trip for her latest effort, in a Listed novice hurdle at Exeter, and although she couldn't match the winner Wilde About Oscar there, that winner could be useful and she was 14 lengths clear of the 138-rated Oscar Elite. Granted the latter runner may not have run to that sort of level, but it was still a useful effort from The Glancing Queen on heavy ground and one that entitles her to be competitive in this race where a faster surface and her course experience could stand her in good stead.

The remarkable story of the Shark Hanlon-trained **Skyace** looks set to continue with a dream appearance for her connections in this race. Bought for just £600 out of the Willie Mullins yard last summer, she has won four of her eight races, including Listed and Grade 3 contests, at odds of 66/1 and 28/1, on her last two starts.

The massive price at Down Royal was on account of her four defeats in a row going into a race with the likes of Queens Brook, Brave Way and Politesse. The leaders went fast up front that day and she came through strongly late on to beat Queens Brook, last year's Champion Bumper third. Naturally, plenty thought she got lucky there, given the way the race turned out, but she proved it was no fluke when she gave weight away to all seven of her rivals in the new Listed Voler La Vedette Mares Novice Hurdle at Punchestown (Minella Melody won it last year).

The form of that race – Global Equity was back in fourth and a useful Willie Mullins mare Finest Evermore was third – has worked out well and she is probably underrated again here. This has been her target ever since and the absence of 102 days isn't a big concern considering she won on her seasonal debut for her new yard, coming off a 302-day absence.

Of the remaining Willie Mullins team, the nicely bred pair **Glens Of Antrim** and **Pont Aval** are interesting. Glens Of Antrim is still a maiden after three starts but has met some useful types like Stattler and Mr Incredible. She is a full sister to the classy Minella Melody, sent off favourite for this race last year, and could well improve on her fourth start.

Pont Aval is a half-sister to Pont Alexandre, but has had plenty of problems it seems given she is an eight-year-old and only got off the mark over hurdles at Punchestown last month.

Allavina and **Martello Sky** are two mares who have been able to reel off a few wins and both come into this in good form, but will have to step up significantly on what they have achieved so far.

Conclusion

There is very little between the Irish mares at the top of the market and while Royal Kahala is probably the standout form pick, it would only be a marginal call. With that in mind, it may be worth taking a chance on Skyace, underrated for both of her big wins this season, but one that should be treated with respect now. (Ronan)

Skyace (Royal Kahala)

Day Four

Look for horses who performed well in a Graded race last time out – 14 of the last 21 winners won or were placed. Winners do well here – eight of the last 12 winners were unbeaten. Nicky Henderson has a good record – he has won the race seven times.

When it comes to choosing between a horse that has shown form on the bridle and one that has shown it can battle, especially in a championship race at the Cheltenham Festival, I have found it pays to side with the latter.

There have been plenty of examples of the toughie getting the better of the cruiser, none more so than when Hardy Eustace got the better of Harchibald in the 2005 Champion Hurdle.

That was a long time ago, but in more recent years we've seen plenty of horses grind it out up that daunting climb to the line.

This year the Triumph Hurdle market is headed by two very useful performers.

The current favourite is **Zanahiyr**, a son of Nathaniel who was bred by the Aga Khan to run on the Flat.

He ran four times in that sphere, sixth in his only start at two and then three times at three, winning a 1m 4f maiden at Fairyhouse in July 2020. To his credit he battled on well to win there, beating a horse now rated on 80 by one and a quarter lengths.

Moved from Mick Halford to former trainer Gordon Elliott, he again had to dig deep to get the better of Dark Voyager on his hurdling debut at Ballinrobe in October.

The following month he put up an improved display in a Grade 3 at Fairyhouse, jumping fluently and coming away easily to beat the odds-on Saint Sam by 14 lengths.

His next appearance came in the Grade 2 Knight Frank Juvenile Hurdle at Leopardstown over Christmas. Well supported at 1/2, he challenged on the bridle at the second last and went away on the run-in to beat Busselton by three and three-quarter lengths.

There is an upward trajectory to this horse's form. A big horse with scope, he has won his last two races with greater ease than his earlier ones despite facing stronger opposition. He jumps very well and seems an uncomplicated ride.

Tritonic may end up edging out Zanahiyr for the top spot at the head of the market.

He was the better of the two on the Flat, winning two of his three starts at two including the prestigious Haynes, Hanson & Clark Stakes at Newbury, before finishing fifth in the Group 3 Zetland Stakes.

Last season started with an excellent half-length second to Highland Chief in the Golden Gates Handicap at Royal Ascot, followed by a second in a Listed race at Hamilton and the same spot in a 0-100 at Yarmouth. His season ended with a fourth place in a valuable 1m 4f Class 2 handicap at Newmarket.

Zanahiyr didn't have a mark on the Flat, but on lines through those he beat he would probably have been allocated something in the mid to high 80s, up against Tritonic's mark of 99.

Tritonic started his hurdling career at Ascot in January. Settled in fourth, his jumping was slick and efficient – just a little big at the third and close to the fifth – and he turned for home in third about five lengths behind the leader.

For much of the straight he looked held by Casa Loupi until halfway up the run-in he responded to his rider's urgings to get up close home, a length clear at the line.

Just over a month later he ran in the Grade 2 Adonis Hurdle at Kempton.

I had misgivings beforehand about his suitability to the track, especially on the good ground, but these proved unfounded.

Travelling strongly just off the pace, he tapped the top of the fifth and was close to the last two, but he was always travelling strongly and quickened away halfway up the run-in to beat Ascot rival Casa Loupi by 10 lengths.

We don't have much to go on, but Tritonic probably has a better turn of foot than Zanahiyr and he has the greater experience.

Having said that they are two progressive young hurdlers with the attributes required to win a Triumph Hurdle. They both travel well through a race, jump proficiently and have shown they can find reserves to come up the hill.

Quilixios comes from a different background.

Unraced on the Flat, he won a three-year-old hurdle by 12 lengths in France in March before joining former trainer Gordon Elliott in the summer.

Now with Henry de Bromhead, he was ridden prominently to win at Punchestown and Down Royal in October, landing short odds both times, before stepping up in class for a Grade 1 juvenile hurdle at Leopardstown in February. Jumping well, he lobbed along in third until taking the lead on the turn for home to beat Saint Sam and Busselton by five and a half lengths and ten and a quarter lengths.

Saint Sam had previously been beaten twice by Zanahiyr, by 14 lengths and six lengths, while Busselton had run Zanahiyr to three and three-quarter lengths over Christmas.

Zanahiyr possibly has a slight edge over his stable companion if the form is taken literally but in essence there is probably not much between them.

One of the toughest juvenile hurdlers we've seen this season is **Adagio**.

David Pipe's German-bred was bought after winning a 1m 4f claimer at Clairefontaine in August. He made his hurdling debut for this yard at Warwick in November, overcoming a clumsy last-flight blunder to beat Duke Of Condicote by a comfortable margin.

The following month he was raised in class for a Grade 2 at Cheltenham but despite running well he was unable to hold the gutsy Duffle Coat. He went back there in December for a Class 2 and returned to winning ways, pulling clear of Historic Heart after the last, before keeping on strongly to beat Nassalam in the Grade 1 Finale Hurdle at Chepstow.

Adagio loves to win and has winning course experience to his name. His hurdling mark is just 2lb adrift of Tritonic yet he can be backed at five times the price. His tenacity and experience will stand him in good stead.

Duffle Coat, unbeaten in four starts over hurdles, has not been seen out since beating Adagio in November. The grey never makes things look easy but he is extremely tough and has a strong finish. He is, though, reported to be an unlikely runner.

Stable companion **Teahupoo**, a winner of a 2m 2f hurdle in France in October and then twice for this yard at Fairyhouse, may also miss the meeting.

He won on his Irish debut by 15 lengths and then beat Tax For Max by seven lengths in February.

Busselton is held by Quilixios and Zanahiyr. Rated on 133, Joseph O'Brien has the option of aiming him at the Boodles.

Haut En Couleurs, a winner of a 2m 2f hurdle in heavy ground at Auteuil, has not yet run for Willie Mullins. The 15-length third in that race, Magic Dream, has subsequently won twice over fences, notably a Grade 2 last time out.

Whatever plans the trainer has this is a name to note.

Dual Fontwell winner **Nassalam** has subsequently finished behind Adagio and **Monmiral**. The latter is unbeaten in four starts, in France last March and then at Exeter in November, Doncaster in December and last time at Haydock.

He was most impressive at Haydock, jumping well, but he is not in the race. A supplementary entry would make him of great interest.

Conclusion

One never knows how things are going to turn out, but my initial impression is that this is a decent Triumph Hurdle.

The four at the top of the market are unbeaten in 10 races, winning more often than not by wide margins.

My long-term fancy for this, since I first heard he was going hurdling, has been Tritonic.

I always liked him on the Flat and Alan King, who has had some top-class juveniles through his hands, says this is the most highly rated horse that he has put over hurdles. His owners are closely linked to the meeting through their IT firm Ultima and they would dearly love to get a winner here.

Zanahiyr may struggle to match Tritonic's tenacity and turn of foot from the last, while Quilixios may spend just a little too much time in the air.

Of the others Adagio is a safe pair of hands, but I want to stay loyal to Tritonic. (Marten)

Tritonic (Adagio)

The Albert Bartlett Novices' Hurdle Race (Grade 1)
abt 3m

2.30

Hurdle winning form is important as ten of the last 12 winners had won at least twice over hurdles. Avoid horses aged five – despite 45 runners, only one has obliged since the race became a Grade 1.

The betting for this 3m test reflects the open nature of the race.

Willie Mullins favours this over the Ballymore for **Stattler**, who was prominent for a long way in the Grade 1 won by Gaillard Du Mesnil at Leopardstown last month. Before that he had run third in a 2m 3f maiden hurdle at Naas and next time won over 2m 4f at Leopardstown. A useful bumper performer, this son of Stowaway has finished in the first three in each of his six starts and he is a half-brother to Binge Drinker, a winner over three miles.

Fakiera has an awkward way of galloping – he's all legs and arms – and he carries his head quite high too, but there is something immensely likeable about him.

He's no star and falls short in the speed department, but he will relish this 3m – two furlongs further than he has ever been before.

He was two lengths behind Stattler in that Grade 1 at Leopardstown staying on strongly from the home turn. The six-year-old, formerly trained by Gordon Elliott, also came home well in each of his previous six runs over hurdles and did well to win over the minimum two miles at Fairyhouse in November. He won next time over 2m 4f but everything about him points to his needing a proper test of stamina.

This race favours horses with experience rather than lightly raced sorts and although there will be classier types in the field rest assured, from what I have seen, this gawky French-bred will run his heart out to the line.

His stable companion **Torygraph** also stays well. He failed to win in four bumper starts, but he won over hurdles in good style at Fairyhouse and Thurles over 2m 7f having finished second on his hurdling debut over a shorter trip. He seems well suited to testing ground.

Farouk D'alene, from the same yard, has an entry for the Martin Pipe. He was beaten by Fakiera at Navan and doesn't jump well.

Barbados Buck's warrants his place in the field. Well held in two bumpers, he's won three of his four starts since switching to hurdles, all over the extended three miles. He showed when just getting the better of Fantastikas at Southwell that he's a lazy sort who does the minimum required to win.

Paul Nicholls rates stable companion **Threeunderthrufive** on a par with Barbados Buck's but he stands at twice the price.

He is unbeaten in three starts over hurdles, at Lingfield, Ludlow and last time over 3m at Musselburgh. The six-year-old doesn't do a lot when he strikes the front but that's not a bad thing around here in a field of this size. There was talk of his missing this meeting for Aintree.

Fergal O'Brien's **Alaphilippe** looks a useful recruit. The seven-year-old needed four runs before winning an Irish point-to-point on his fifth outing but he made an immediate impression upon joining this yard, winning a Ffos Las bumper in October and then three of his four starts over hurdles.

He had some fair performers behind him on his latest outing at Haydock and we've not seen the best of him yet.

Adrimel was beaten 40 lengths in the bumper here last March but he has since been unbeaten in three starts over hurdles, the last two on heavy ground. At Warwick in January he gave 3lb to a horse rated 3lb better but that was over 2m 5f and I'm not sure about him over this longer trip.

Mahler Allstar, not disgraced when finishing in mid-division in the bumper here last season, shaped well when third to Stattler over 2m 4f in December. He's 66/1 and can outrun those odds.

The Cob, who needs to be supplemented, would warrant a look. Ben Pauling's son of Let The Lion Roar has won three from six, notably last time winning an extended 3m Grade 2 at Doncaster by nine lengths. He's tough but may prefer testing ground.

N'golo has four other entries for the meeting, including the Martin Pipe and Coral Cup, but those close to the horse believe he has more to offer. This trip may be beyond him.

Hereford winner **Bothwell Bridge** won over an extended 3m 1f at Hereford by 39 lengths despite racing keenly in the early stages. His stamina is assured but this will be harder.

Ashdale Bob beat Fakiera by six lengths in a Grade 2 at Navan in December but he fell in Bob Olinger's race at Naas and was then beaten a long way by Gaillard Du Mesnil at Leopardstown, finishing behind Stattler and Fakiera.

Streets Of Doyen has plenty of experience, winning four of his 11 starts over hurdles, having won over the Old Course here in October. Decent ground would suit him.

The mare **Atlantic Fairy** receives 7lb but connections may prefer to save her for Fairyhouse. She would be a likely contender for the lead if this were her chosen option.

Conclusion

Even on decent ground this can prove an attritional test and I would rather have an assured battler with a few runs to his name than one that is lightly raced.

As you will have gathered I believe Fakiera has the attributes required to win here. Obviously there is the concern over the yard, but at around 7/1 – with four places available – I expect him to make the frame.

Next best is Barbados Buck's, who probably has more to offer. (Marten)

Fakiera (Barbados Buck's)

The WellChild Cheltenham Gold Cup Steeple Chase (Grade 1)
3m abt 2½f

3.05

Recent winning form is important here – 16 of the last 20 winners won last time out and this is the same stat when it comes to winners that have won or been placed at the Festival previously. Avoid horses that have run a lot this season – only two of the last 19 winners ran more than three times that season.

There are those who say there is no such thing as a poor Gold Cup but looking back at last year's running there is a case for suggesting it was far from being a vintage renewal.

The 2020 Gold Cup was generally considered beforehand as the most open for many years, a view subsequently confirmed by the sight of six horses in close contention approaching the final fence, with a couple more snapping at their heels.

One can't knock the winner Al Boum Photo because he's won his only subsequent start but those behind him have hardly shone.

Santini, beaten a neck, has been beaten three times, on the last two occasions by 10 lengths in the King George and then 17 lengths by Native River at Sandown.

Lostintranslation, who was a length and a half away in third, has been beaten 47 lengths, 26 lengths and pulled up from three starts.

Fourth home Monalee was third in his only subsequent outing while the fifth Delta Work has been beaten twice and once unseated. Real Steel, now with Paul Nicholls, was third at Ascot before pulling up in the King George. Clan Des Obeaux has been beaten in his three subsequent starts and Chris's Dream has been beaten twice.

On a more positive note Kemboy, 12 lengths behind, was twice beaten before winning the Irish Gold Cup at Leopardstown while Bristol De Mai won the Betfair Chase on his return and then ran second to Native River at Sandown.

Of course Al Boum Photo could do no more than beat the horses put before him, but the fact that last year's runner-up Santini and third home Lostintranslation are now priced at 14/1 and 33/1 respectively suggests this year's race is stronger.

In winning **Al Boum Photo** became only the eighth horse in the race's history to win it more than once – and the first to do so since Kauto Star in 2009.

Yet the eight-year-old, a son of Buck's Boum – a full brother to Big Buck's – has not caught the public imagination in the way that past dual winners have.

Perhaps that is down to the fact that we have seen so little of him. He ran only once before this victory and just twice prior to his 2019 triumph.

Willie Mullins has stuck with his tried and tested formula again, with the horse appearing at Tramore on New Year's Day where he beat stable companion Acapella Bourgeois by 19 lengths.

The public want a story, be it a human subplot or a touch of equine brilliance, and we just don't seem to have that with Al Boum Photo, which is a shame because he has a thoroughly likeable way of going about his business.

Al Boum Photo enjoyed a relatively smooth passage through the field when winning the race for the first time in 2019. Held up in arrears in the early stages, he made steady progress into fourth turning for home and took the lead at the last to pull clear and hold the strong-finishing Anibale Fly by two and a half lengths. His jumping was, for the most part, safe and assured without being spectacular.

We saw little of him last season – just the one appearance in the same Tramore chase (upgraded to Grade 3) he won the previous year, when he beat a rival rated 23lb inferior by six lengths – but that was always the plan, with Willie Mullins keen to replicate the 2018/19 campaign.

The story of the winner's 2020 Gold Cup triumph is simply told.

Settled from flagfall on the outside of the field, he was soon in mid-division and jumping efficiently. His one serious mistake came at the 13th but it didn't cost him any momentum. Taking the lead four fences from home, he was joined by Santini before putting in his best jump at the last, thereby securing an advantage of more than the neck by which he won.

Afterwards Paul Townend said the horse "missed a few fences" but there was no doubting his tenacity from the last.

The horse's record is hard to fault, but surely this is a stronger field than last year and improvement will be required?

If there was an unlucky horse in last year's race it was probably **Santini**, who went down by a diminishing neck after having to be switched twice from the penultimate fence.

Those manoeuvres cost him more than his margin of defeat yet he was still able to put in a power-packed finish, one which would have seen him prevail in another few strides.

Third to Kilbricken Storm in the 2018 Albert Bartlett Novices' Hurdle at Cheltenham before winning the Grade 1 Doom Bar Sefton Novices' Hurdle at Aintree, he made a belated start to chasing when winning an extended 2m 7f Grade 2 contest on his seasonal return at Newbury in December 2018.

Next time out he stayed on very late in the day to finish a never-nearer third to the gutsy La Bague Au Roi and Topofthegame in the Kauto Star Novices' Chase at Kempton on Boxing Day before again finding Topofthegame half a length too good for him in the RSA Insurance Novices' Chase at Cheltenham.

On that occasion Santini's chance was compromised by a few untidy jumps out in the country, notably at the fourth last, as well as by an interrupted preparation due to the equine flu outbreak which caused him to miss his preparatory run in the Reynoldstown Chase.

He also pulled off a shoe during a racecourse gallop, leaving him lame and sore on the Tuesday of the week before the meeting, only becoming sound a day or two before the race.

His trainer said the horse came out of Cheltenham in better shape than he had been going into it, and although consideration was given to Aintree they opted instead to protect him with the future in mind.

The son of Milan is a safe but slightly hesitant jumper. He measures the fences with precision, arching his back rather than having a cut. He is, though, a thorough stayer, as he showed when wresting back the lead from Bristol De Mai in the Cotswold Chase at Cheltenham last January.

That run had followed a hard-fought defeat of a horse rated 19lb inferior in a 3m Listed race at Sandown in November when, to put it bluntly, he looked slow. Henderson had the horse's palate cauterised after the race.

The trainer actually used the word 'slow' when discussing the horse's work at home after Sandown, adding that he thrives on hard graft.

Sheepskins were called upon in the Gold Cup and they have been used in his three starts this season.

On his return at Aintree he was outbattled by Lake View Lad, where the fences in the straight were omitted, before looking very one-paced when fifth to Frodon in the King George. Last time on heavy ground at Sandown he was beaten 17 lengths by Native River after a couple of mistakes.

Given the way Nicky Henderson trains his top horses I expect Santini to run his best race of the season in the Gold Cup. The track, likely good ground and strong pace will suit him but he does not appear to have an edge over his rivals and, if anything, he seems to have regressed.

In a Gold Cup where it was hard to call the winner from the home turn, **Lostintranslation** appeared to hold as good a chance as any.

Bravely ridden around the inside by Robbie Power, the eight-year-old jumped best of the leading contenders and came to the last holding every chance. One could hardly say he didn't stay, but he didn't find as much as the first two up the climb to the line, a performance consistent with his pedigree which has a bottom line comprised mainly of Flat performers.

A useful novice hurdler, who ran Black Op to half a length in the Grade 1 Betway Mersey Novices' Hurdle at Aintree in the spring of 2018, he took well to fences the following autumn, jumping confidently on his first two starts behind La Bague Au Roi, before rallying gamely to beat Defi Du Seuil in the Grade 2 Dipper Novices' Chase over an extended 2m 4f at Cheltenham on New Year's Day 2019.

He then found that rival just too strong for him, both in the Grade 1 Scilly Isles Novices' Chase at Sandown and the Grade 1 JLT Novices' Chase at Cheltenham, before showing his appreciation for the step up to 3m 1f when beating Topofthegame by six lengths in the Grade 1 Betway Mildmay Novices' Chase at Aintree.

Things moved on again last autumn, with a comfortable victory in a 2m 4f Listed race at Carlisle, where the feature of his performance was an exceptional round of jumping, before a rather more workmanlike victory over Bristol De Mai in the Betfair Chase at Haydock.

On that occasion Lostintranslation had to dig deep to win, but he beat a horse that has made Haydock his own in recent years and it resulted in a 12lb rise in his rating from 161 to 173.

The eight-year-old's next assignment came in the King George VI Chase at Kempton.

Keen in the early stages, his jumping lacked its customary fluency but he was still on the bridle passing the winning post as they embarked upon the second circuit before signs appeared that Robbie Power was starting to become restless. His mount then came back on the bridle before a couple of ponderous jumps cost him ground and by the turn for home he was beaten.

A few days after the race, Lostintranslation had his palate cauterised and he went to Cheltenham wearing a tongue-tie.

Colin Tizzard's stable did not enjoy a good week at Cheltenham so, in the circumstances, the horse ran with great credit.

This season has not gone well, with defeats in the Betfair Chase, pulled up in the King George after breaking a blood vessel and then, following wind surgery, a 26-length fifth of seven to Secret Investor at Newbury.

In fairness he ran well for a long way at Newbury, travelling smoothly in arrears and putting in some fine leaps. Passing the post on the first circuit he was still moving comfortably within himself and three fences from home, jumping the open ditch, he looked the likely winner but by the second last he had emptied, stopping as if something were badly amiss.

He needs to improve on last year's form but on the evidence to hand he has actually deteriorated. Having said that he still travels through his races like a good horse and if the trainer and his team can resolve his problem, which is evidently physical, he could run well.

The horse with the market momentum behind him is **Champ**.

The son of King's Theatre has come a long way since his younger days, starting with a debut success at Southwell in January 2017, and a maiden hurdle success three starts later over our club horse, Court Dreaming, at Perth in May 2018.

He won five of his seven starts over hurdles, finding City Island two lengths too good for him in the 2019 Ballymore Novices' Hurdle, but has subsequently attained a higher level of form over fences, winning each of his completed starts last season culminating in an extraordinary success in the RSA Novices' Chase at Cheltenham, where he made up the best part of 10 lengths from the last to beat Minella Indo and Allaho, pulling away at the line.

Champ was keen to get on with things at Cheltenham, but Barry Geraghty did a good job settling him despite his mount's rather ponderous technique over the fences. In fact the only fence where he noticeably made headway was the fourth last in a display of jumping that was consistent with his first three runs.

It says much for his class that he was able to produce such a strong surge at the finish despite having, at that time, a flawed jumping technique.

We saw a much more assured performer on his belated return to action in February.

Intriguingly asked to drop to an extended two miles – a trip that he had never covered either over hurdles or fences – he ran in the Grade 2 Game Spirit Chase and, in finishing two lengths behind the specialist two-miler Sceau Royal, he exceeded my expectations.

Striding along at the head of affairs he jumped with a hitherto unseen confidence, looking keen to go faster down the back straight. Still leading on the turn for home, he put in his best jump of the race at the third last and only gave way to the winner approaching the last.

At no stage did his rider resort to the whip as he went down by two lengths, conceding the winner 3lb.

As for his stamina his dam is a half-sister to triple Gold Cup winner Best Mate and long-distance winners Cornish Rebel and Inca Trail and the way he finished in the RSA should put any concerns on that score to rest.

Champ is apparently very relaxed at home – you can see something of that in his races – and he may just have been a slow learner.

Champ will go to Cheltenham a fresh horse, on the back of an excellent run and with course experience to call upon. His mark of 165 is 10lb behind Al Boum Photo and 5lb below Santini, but of all the horses in this year's field he is the one with the most potential to improve.

Now that his jumping is more assured he has a leading chance.

The other with the scope to progress is **A Plus Tard**.

Henry de Bromhead's seven-year-old has proved exceptionally consistent throughout his career, never finishing out of the first three in 15 starts, on all but three occasions in the first two.

He has twice run at the Festival, powering clear to win the 2019 Close Brothers Novices' Handicap Chase by 16 lengths from a mark of 144 and then last year sticking on well to finish third to Min in the Ryanair over an extended 2m4f.

Third to Delta Work in a Grade 1 at Punchestown in April 2019, on his only previous start at three miles, he returned to the trip on his latest start at Leopardstown in the Grade 1 Savills Chase.

Equipped with a tongue-tie for the first time, he travelled well until the home turn, when he came under pressure and looked held. He still seemed to be destined for third after jumping the last until a late and unexpected surge saw him power home and pip Kemboy near the line.

This display certainly augurs well for the longer trip of the Gold Cup, while his experience of the track will stand him in good stead.

A line through Kemboy's form in this race last season leaves him with plenty to find, but that is misleading and his mark of 170 is just 5lb short of the favourite.

He has never in his life run a bad race and he has to command the utmost respect.

The surprise contender in this year's race is **Royale Pagaille**.

There is always one horse that eludes me when I am writing my Gold Cup and Champion Hurdle previews in the autumn, but this horse's exclusion was entirely forgivable given his form last season.

A fair performer in France, where he won a four-year-old hurdle from 10 starts over hurdles and fences, he ran twice for Venetia Williams last season, beaten in a match by Vision Des Flos and then last of three behind Equus Secretus at Huntingdon.

He started this season racing from a mark of 135 – over two stones adrift of a Gold Cup rating – but victories off 135, 140 and then last time by 16 lengths off 156 have seen his mark rise to 166, leaving him within a few pounds of the leading contenders.

Royale Pagaille is not a flawless jumper and he is prone to lug left over a fence. He has only raced on ground described as soft or heavy, both this season and last, but he is sure to stay and comes here with an upward profile.

He was most impressive to the eye last time at Haydock. Lobbing along comfortably within himself, he was always in charge and strode away up the straight to win without coming off the bridle.

The chief concern for his supporters will be the prospect of better ground. There is no evidence to suggest that he won't handle it – indeed the progeny of his sire Blue Bresil are suited by all types of ground – but clearly a few heavy showers would be welcomed by the yard.

Kemboy's jumping, which let him down when he unseated at the first here in 2019, has been a cause for concern.

He ended the 2019 campaign with two notable victories, beating Clan Des Obeaux by nine lengths in the Betway Bowl Chase at Aintree having travelled well before quickening away on the run-in, and then beating Al Boum Photo by two lengths in the Punchestown Gold Cup, staying on strongly from the last.

The eight-year-old has plenty of speed for a staying chaser, to such an extent that he sometimes races freely, but his eagerness to get on with things leaves him short of reserves for the finish.

He does, though, tend to jump rather flat over the fences. He seldom gets round without clouting a fence at some point and he had not looked entirely happy around the course when fourth to Shattered Love in the 2018 JLT Novices' Chase.

It was the same story in last year's Gold Cup, when a series of sloppy jumps cost him ground, but to his credit he still travelled smoothly through the race and came home quite well.

This season he performed with credit when runner-up to Presenting Percy at Thurles and then when caught in the last couple of strides at Leopardstown over Christmas.

He looked right back to his best when beating The Storyteller by a couple of lengths in the Irish Gold Cup. Setting off in front and jumping for fun, he stayed on strongly all the way to the line.

There were no signs of the mistakes which blighted Kemboy's earlier races at Leopardstown but Cheltenham may not be his track. His form figures here read 54U7 and I would not be sure of his getting home up the hill over the Gold Cup trip.

He is, though, coming here in tip-top form and with a clear round he could be a contender.

There would be no more popular winner than **Frodon.**

This admirable performer seems to have been around for ages yet he's only nine and there may still be improvement to come.

His superb jumping stands him in good stead and the season before last he ran on with great tenacity to beat Aso in the Ryanair Chase. He tackled that race again last spring but finished fourth, 15 lengths behind Min, on ground that was softer than ideal.

Frodon won the Cotswold Chase over the extended 3m 1f in January 2019, and he beat West Approach under top weight on his return over the 3m 1f of the Old Course.

This season he has progressed to a whole new level, starting with a comfortable defeat of West Approach in that 3m 1f handicap here in October and then last time making all to win the King George VI Chase at Kempton by two and a quarter lengths from Waiting Patiently.

I am prepared to ignore his run at Aintree in December when the absence of the fences in the straight played against his main strength.

The Gold Cup is over the extended 3m 2f and although he has won over a furlong short of that distance, in the 2019 Cotswold Chase, given his exuberant style of racing that trip may just prove beyond him.

Also he may not get as easy a time in front as he did at Kempton. He has, though, now won six times at the track and he is admirably ridden by Bryony Frost. Good ground suits him well.

Minella Indo is a natural over fences.

In last year's RSA he was allowed to lob along at the head of affairs with Allaho, his sound jumping ensuring that he remained competitive. He was especially impressive at the open ditches with his one error coming at the final fence. Despite that, he was just getting the better of Allaho only to get caught close home by Champ.

This season everything went well on his first two starts at Wexford and Navan, up with the pace both times and pulling clear to win comfortably at the line.

He had the first fall of his career next time in the Savills Chase at Leopardstown before running a disappointing race in the Irish Gold Cup, finding less than expected after the last to fade back to fourth.

That form isn't good enough to win a Gold Cup, and the eight-year-old has not yet won in Grade 1 company. However he's made the frame in all but one of his 11 completed starts – the other time was when fourth to Kemboy – and he has a likeable way of going.

Allaho also enjoyed himself in the RSA, jumping well in the main and staying on all the way to the line to be beaten just a couple of lengths by the winner.

The son of No Risk At All has come up against Minella Indo a few times, beating him on his hurdling debut in February 2019 and then twice finishing behind him at Cheltenham and Punchestown before running a length behind him in the RSA.

This season two defeats at Punchestown and Leopardstown were followed by a three-length victory in a 2m 4f Grade 2 at Thurles. It wasn't a convincing display – he made mistakes at the last two fences – and Willie Mullins seems to favour the Ryanair.

Nobody would begrudge the 11-year-old **Native River** winning the race for a second time, although the last horse of that age or older to win the race was What A Myth, who won as a 12-year-old for Ryan Price in 1969.

Native River was rated on 166 when he beat Might Bite in that epic duel in 2018 and was far from disgraced when fourth to Al Boum Photo a year later. Since then he has won three of his four starts, all Grade 2 races, at Aintree and Newbury and then a third to Lake View Lad back at Aintree in December.

He looked as good as ever last time at Sandown, relishing the heavy ground to beat Bristol De Mai by nine and a half lengths with Santini back in third.

He is now rated on 172, 5lb higher than a year ago and just 4lb short of the mark he received after winning his Gold Cup.

The softer the ground the better it will suit him, but he can handle better ground – it was good when he beat Secret Investor last February – and his extraordinary tenacity and will to win will ensure he is a factor. He is rated just 3lb behind the favourite. History, though, is stacked up against him.

Imperial Aura has not been seen out since unseating his rider at Kempton in January. He looks more likely to run in the Ryanair.

Stable companion **Vinndication** ran very creditably when chasing home Cyrname in the Charlie Hall but then unseated his rider in the Ladbrokes Trophy at Newbury. He's not been seen out since.

Melon has an admirable Festival record – runner-up in a Supreme, two Champion Hurdles and beaten a nose by Samcro in last year's Marsh Novices' Chase. This trip looks beyond him.

Conclusion

It's an old racing cliché, but Al Boum Photo has done nothing wrong. The only concern I have is that last year's form may not be good enough to win this year's race. At odds of 5/2 he makes little appeal.

The ground is unlikely to be testing enough to bring out the best in Native River and Royale Pagaille, but if the heavens should open then expect their odds – currently 16/1 and 10/1 – to be snapped up.

I anticipate market strength building up behind Champ. That was a most encouraging return to action behind a specialist two-miler in the Game Spirit and he powered up the hill last year. I envisage him being a strong second favourite.

A Plus Tard has a similar profile to Champ while Minella Indo needs to put a poor run last time behind him. On last year's RSA form I would give him a chance.

The admirable Frodon may struggle to get home and I suspect the same may apply to Kemboy. Santini could run his best race of the season and at 14/1 he will have his backers even though he is linked into last year's form.

So, too, is Lostintranslation. 33/1 is a big price about a horse with his class but it's a worry to see him finish so weakly. Something seems to have been wrong with him.

To conclude I'm going with Champ. Next best is A Plus Tard. (Marten)

Champ (A Plus Tard)

The St. James's Place Festival Challenge Cup
Open Hunters' Steeple Chase
3m abt 2½f

3.40

The ratings offer a clue here – nine of the last 11 winners were rated 134+. Proven distance form is not needed as none of the last 14 winners had won over this trip. British-bred horses have a terrible record – zero wins despite being represented 81 times over the last 18 years.

At the head of the betting for the second successive year is Willie Mullins' **Billaway**.

Beaten ten lengths by It Came To Pass 12 months ago, he comes here in good form having filled the runner-up spot behind Stand Up And Fight on his seasonal return at Fairyhouse in November, blundering over the final fence but recovering well and rallying close home. He then went on to win twice, firstly on soft ground over an extended 2m 5f at Down Royal in December, comprehensively reversing the form with Stand Up And Fight, beating him over 19 lengths into fifth. He then followed up with a good staying performance to beat Staker Wallace by just over two lengths on heavy ground over 3m 1f at Naas in January.

Jumping hasn't always been Billaway's strong point but he appears to be learning with experience. He's also a strong stayer and travels well in big fields. Take the winner out of last year's race, he beat the rest of the field comfortably and a reproduction of that effort will see him go close again.

Next in is the Paul Nicholls-trained and the David Maxwell-owned **Bob And Co**.

The 10-year-old won twice last season, including over 3m 2f at Fontwell on soft ground, but it was his inability to settle which led connections to swerve this race in favour of the Aintree Foxhunters' Chase over the shorter distance of 2m 5f.

This term we've only seen Bob And Co once which came after a wind operation and resulted in an easy victory over 2m 6f at Haydock, beating a good field including Wishing And Hoping, The Worlds End and Ravished, by 17 lengths under Sean Bowen.

On the little evidence to hand, he appeared more relaxed and saw out his race strongly having made a few jumping errors along the way. Those can be put down to a lack of match practice as throughout his career he has always appeared foot assured.

The highest rated amongst these, he has to have a strong chance. It's just a shame his owner, who bought the horse so he could ride him in this race, won't be able to take the mount.

It Came To Pass provided a memorable day for trainer/daughter combination Eugene and Maxine O'Sullivan 12 months ago when their plucky son of Brian Boru romped to victory at odds of 66/1.

There was no fluke about the result with previous beatings of Billaway and On The Fringe in the book, but a lacklustre preparation on unsuitable testing ground led to him being overlooked. Come the big day, the ground dried out and he travelled and jumped like a dream, relishing the underfoot conditions before sprinting clear up the hill.

Seen twice since, he finished fourth to Stand Up And Fight at Fairyhouse in November, shaping better than the result suggests, before unseating at Thurles in late February when well out of contention.

Both those races were on terrible ground but if conditions came right for him on the day, he certainly can't be discounted lightly.

The winner of that Thurles race was **Jury Duty**. Fresh from a break having finished second to Winged Leader in a point-to-point at Portrush back in October, he travelled and jumped well before idling up the run-in, allowing Stand Up And Fight to close to three parts of a length. Jury Duty has a touch of quality which counts for a lot in this sort of race. He could go well if he gets into a rhythm.

Stand Up And Fight, sixth here in 2019, took advantage of a final fence blunder from Billaway on his reappearance this season at Fairyhouse in November, but that form was comprehensively reversed next time at Down Royal. I'm sure he'll run his race but victory may elude him once more.

Staker Wallace shapes as if he's on the cusp of landing a big prize and ran well here last year on what was only his third start after a mammoth absence. He has won once from four starts this season and finished second in the other three, including last time at Naas when plugging on well behind Billaway. There's little to suggest he can reverse that form, but he has place claims.

Kelly Morgan trained the Sir Johnny Weatherby-owned Top Wood to finish second and third in this race in 2018 and 2019 respectively and looks to go closer this term with **Red Indian** from the same connections.

Fairly useful in his days with Ben Pauling, he finished sixth in the Grade 3 Coral Cup in 2018 before winning a novice chase for current connections later that year. He achieved a career-high mark of 145 in that sphere and wasn't disgraced when fourth to La Bague Au Roi in the Grade 1 Kauto Star Novices' Chase at Kempton before steadily losing form.

Switched to point-to-points in October, he won in a hack canter around Bishops Court for handler Mimi Eggleston before sauntering to a very easy victory at Alnwick in December when back under Kelly Morgan's wing.

Not the easiest to keep sound but evidently in good heart, connections were hoping to run him again in mid-January but with so many cancelled fixtures the decision was made to head straight here. We don't yet know if he will get home over 3m 2f, but he's relatively lightly raced and this has been the plan for a long time.

Another lightly raced horse is **Mr Mantilla** who makes plenty of appeal at a price.

Completely unexposed with only the six starts to his name, he's only a head short of a full set of victories having lost out in a dive to the line in a Lingstown 'winner of two' race over 3m in March. Forced to take an early holiday due to lockdown restrictions, he then reappeared in October to win by a length from a subsequent two-time winner who has since joined Willie Mullins. Mr Mantilla then went on to win twice more with a half-length victory over Rewritetherules followed by a five-length success over the Mullins-trained Bellow Mome.

Extremely likeable with a fantastic attitude to match his sound jumping and his ability to stay. He could be worth taking a chance on.

Tom Ellis' eight-year-old **Latenightpass** sprung a 40/1 surprise when winning a hunter chase at Warwick in February. Unrelenting on the front end, he jumped for fun and had just enough in reserve to hold off the late challenge of Highway Jewel to win by three quarters of a length.

With winning course and distance form from 2019 when he won a 15-runner hunters' chase at Cheltenham's May meeting, it's hard to rule out a bold show despite him needing to find something on ratings with a few of these. He's a lively outsider.

Another eight-year-old with an outside chance is Melanie Rowley's **Salvatore**.

He stayed on strongly to get the better of Alcala at Musselburgh when last seen, jumping well and seeing out the extended 3m 2f in taking fashion. Prior to that he'd won three point-to-points on the trot, beating familiar names in Ballyboker Breeze, Barney Dwan and Coningsby. Back in 2019 he finished third to the aforementioned Latenightpass over this course and distance but seems to have come of age since then.

Hazel Hill was forced to withdraw due to an irregular heartbeat on the morning of last year's race when bidding to defend his crown. Now 13 years old, he's in his twilight years but he wasn't for stopping when staying on strongly to beat Ravished by a widening four and a half lengths at Ludlow in January. That came off the back of being well beaten by Highway Jewel in December but he's entitled to have needed that run and he's not easy to rule out given his perfect record over course and distance.

Joe O'Shea's **Road To Rome** finished fourth to Hazel Hill in the 2019 renewal before filling fifth place in the Aintree Foxhunters'. He recently returned from a 659-day absence at Wetherby but was well beaten into seventh. He's entitled to have needed that but it requires a leap of faith to follow him here.

The winner of that Wetherby race was **Duhallow Tornado**. The nine-year-old finished tailed off in this race 12 months ago but seemed a reformed character in the first-time blinkers, travelling well on the heels of the leaders before picking up the running turning for home and pulling right away between the final two fences.

Mighty Stowaway returned a wide-margin winner of a Tinahely point-to-point in October but was well held when third behind Stand Up And Fight and Billaway at Fairyhouse in November. He goes well fresh but others make more appeal.

Sam Loxton's **Chameron** came home the easy winner of a couple of point-to-points for the late Rose Loxton last year and returned after 12 months off the track to make a winning hunter chase debut at Leicester in February, travelling strongly under Harry Cobden and showing a good attitude to lead after the last having forfeited his advantage with a bad mistake over three from home. That form falls some way short of what's required here, but he's young and improving.

Loxton may also run **Caid Du Berlais**. Very useful on his day, although he never tends to save his best for Cheltenham having pulled up in this race for the last two years. Others are preferred.

The 11-year-old, **Monbeg Gold**, produced a much improved effort when going down fighting behind Silsol at Doncaster when last seen. He showed a tendency to jump to his left there, but there was no denying the heart he showed to battle on the run-in. That was his first start on better ground since finishing second to The Dellercheckout at Ludlow last February and he can go on from here.

Back Bar beat Latenightpass in a point-to-point last February and returned in December with a 15-length defeat of Quinto. Pulled up when last seen at Warwick in February. Others make more appeal.

Leading point-to-point jockey turned trainer, Will Biddick, could saddle **Porlock Bay**. He needs to improve having finished a head second to Sametegal at Wincanton in February, but that was on heavy conditions and he was an impressive point-to-point winner on better ground before that.

At 14 years young **Kruzhlinin** would become the oldest horse in history to win this race. The prolific point-to-pointer returned from a long absence in November and finished second to Some Man in a point-to-point at Tinahely before going on to be fourth at Mainstown, on both occasions unsuited to the testing ground. Despite his age, he could outrun his odds if the ground dried out.

Law Of Gold came here in better form 12 months ago but could only manage seventh place. He looks up against it again. **Ravished** is a sight to behold with his bold jumping but he's held by a couple of these. Better ground would aid his chance and he'll give you a run for your money. **Solomn Grundy** always runs his race but usually comes up short, **Wishing And Hoping** was well beaten by Bob And Co last time whilst **Sonneofpresenting** makes up the numbers.

Conclusion

Willie Mullins' Billaway makes obvious appeal with his recent form teamed with his decent second in this race 12 months ago. However, I'm going to take him on with the completely unexposed Mr Mantilla. There's much to like about this seven-year-old, not least his nearly perfect record but also his attitude, the way he goes through a race and his form.

Of the others, Bob And Co appears to be more relaxed during his races which will help him get home whilst Red Indian could go one place better for Kelly Morgan who came close with Top Wood here in 2018 and 2019. (Jodie)

Mr Mantilla (Bob And Co, Red Indian)

The Mrs Paddy Power Mares' Steeple Chase
2m abt ½f

4.15

No stats.

Since mares' races were added to the Cheltenham Festival, namely the Mares' Hurdle and Mares' Novices' Hurdle, Willie Mullins has dominated, winning 14 of the collective 18 renewals of both contests.

It's no surprise that the Irish champion trainer holds the first two in the betting for the inaugural running of the Mares' Chase, and with six of the 19 entries in total, he has a strong chance of getting off to the perfect start in the history of this Grade 2 contest.

Elimay is the favourite and she deserves to be. Lightly raced last season, she looked good when she did run, comfortably beating useful mares Agusta Gold and Cut The Mustard, at Grade 3 and Grade 2 level respectively. She would have been a player in any of the Grade 1 novice chases at Cheltenham but missed the meeting, presumably in favour of a Grade 2 mares' novice chase at Limerick which never happened due to Covid.

She didn't get this season off to the best of starts when managing to lose out to stablemate Buildmeupbuttercup by a nose – a scarce occurrence given that mare's tendency to idle badly in front – in a Listed mares' hurdle at Punchestown, but it was over fences that she impressed last season and she showed she had taken a significant step forward when pushing stablemate Allaho all the way in the Grade 2 Horse & Jockey Hotel Chase over two and a half miles at Thurles, the pair of them all of 79 lengths away from the third. Allaho is probably just short of Grade 1 class, but still holds a rating of 160 and was only conceding Elimay 2lbs, so it was a big run from her.

She booked her ticket for this race with a smooth win over Shattered Love, to whom she was conceding 5lbs, in the Listed Opera Hat Mares' Chase at Naas. That was over a distance of two miles, which is probably on the short side for her (and the runner-up as well) but she jumped well, travelled smoothly and won under just hands and heels.

She is three from four over fences and has the scope to go further than her current Irish rating of 155 (which would probably be inflated further in Britain). That makes her the one to beat.

Colreevy is unbeaten in three starts over fences and is already a Grade 1 winner, courtesy of her win over Pencilfulloflead in the Matchbook Betting Exchange Novice Chase at Limerick over Christmas.

She was a good novice hurdler last season and finished second to Minella Melody in the Grade 3 Solerina Mares' Novice Hurdle at Fairyhouse before finishing fifth to Concertista in the Mares' Novices' Hurdle at Cheltenham. Given she was a very good bumper mare – she beat Abacadabras in the Grade 1 Punchestown

Champion Bumper – you wouldn't have blamed connections for persisting with her over hurdles, especially given her value and the added risk that comes with chasing (she is owned by a breeding family). However she has certainly repaid the decision to take on fences and her win at Limerick was an excellent performance, even if Asterion Forlonge's fall made that race an easier heat.

Having led or shared the lead for much of that 2m 3f contest, she blundered badly at the second last and it should have been race over, but there was so much to like about the way she got back up to beat Pencilfulloflead, a very useful operator on heavy ground and who had beaten Latest Exhibition on his previous start.

Colreevy warmed up for this with a comfortable win in a two-and-a-half-mile Grade 2 novice chase at Thurles. It was interesting after that contest that Willie Mullins alluded that her owners might be keen to stay at home and go for a Grade 2 mares' novice chase at Limerick and he mentioned that again in a press Zoom call recently. Reading between the lines, it sounds like the trainer is keen to go but the owner is not so sure, so that is worth monitoring as her participation in this race is clearly significant.

The other factor to note is that she has to carry a Grade 1 penalty which is unfortunate because she'll have to concede weight all around, though only 2lbs to Elimay, who on paper is her biggest rival.

Another one of her big rivals has to be **Shattered Love**, who of course won over this exact course and distance when she took a brilliant renewal of the Marsh Novices' Chase in 2018 (subsequent Grade 1 winners Terrefort, Kemboy and Finian's Oscar in behind). She went on to lose out to only Al Boum Photo in the Ryanair Novice Chase at Fairyhouse and has since raced in a Cheltenham Gold Cup and Irish Grand National.

She probably hasn't lived up to the promise she showed in her novice year but she has still been a very good mare and most of her good performances have come over two and a half miles (she was a very easy winner of the Listed T.A Morris Memorial Mares Chase over that distance at Thurles for the second year running in November). With that in mind, I think she ran a huge race when second to Elimay in the two-mile Opera Hat on her latest start.

She raced up front that day, in a likely tactical ploy to make her stamina count for more over the shorter distance, but there is only so fast you can go without compromising your own chance and she got tapped for toe by Elimay and Yukon Lil heading into the straight. That she was able to pick up again late in the day, going back past Yukon Lil for a clear second, was testament to her.

The return to the course and distance of the best run of her life plus the fact she will receive weight off Elimay and Colreevy makes her a really interesting proposition, even at the age of ten now.

Annie Mc looks clear best of the home team. Second on both of her point-to-point starts in Ireland (to Honeysuckle on her debut at Dromahane), she did well to get to a mark of 140 over hurdles, and has improved for chasing, especially this season. She reeled off three wins in small-field mares' novice chases going into the Marsh Novices' Chase last season and she was travelling okay in that race before a bad mistake at the fence before the top of the hill, which was as much a reason as any for the long distance she was beaten.

She struggled to make a real impact in a couple of competitive handicap chases on her first two starts this season but benefited from dropping back to mares' company when first beating the useful Cut The Mustard by 16 lengths in a Listed contest at Doncaster and then she comfortably held the measure of Zambella and Happy Diva in another Listed mares' chase at Warwick.

That latest effort was a clear career best and on that she has to have a chance, but this is a step back into a higher class against these quality Irish mares, and I have a slight concern about the track for her.

It's 16/1 bar the top four but there are a couple of interesting mares, perhaps none more so than **Agusta Gold**. She struggled to live with Elimay twice last season but she ran a huge race off a mark of 134 to be second in the Punchestown Irish Grand National Trial on her final start of the campaign.

She began this campaign with a win at Fairyhouse, where she beat the useful Moyhenna, who was in good form at the time, with disappointing Salsaretta in behind them. That was over two miles and five furlongs and she showed her staying capability that day. She did spurn what looked a good opportunity over hurdles off a mark of 125 in a Grade B contest at Navan but she seems to be a much better chaser these days.

The most interesting angle to her is that she has moved to Willie Mullins' yard from Mags Mullins. That only came to light when the entries for this race came out and presumably is because of a change of ownership.

It may be that Agusta Gold is being primed for a run in something like the Irish Grand National later in the season but she'd be really interesting if she was allowed to take her chance in this race.

The same sort of sentiment applies to **Magic Of Light**, whose season has revolved around a return to the Aintree Grand National, given her excellent second in that race in 2019.

Her route to that contest is well worn now. She made it three wins in a row in the same Listed mares' chase at Newbury this season before finishing second to Roksana in a Grade 2 mares' hurdle at Ascot – a race she had won on her previous two starts.

To me, she hasn't looked as good as she has previously in those races – for instance she had 21lbs in hand of the runner-up Sensulano on official ratings at Newbury and she was simply no match for Roksana at Ascot, albeit that mare has had an excellent season.

You could apply the same sort of comment to **Happy Diva**, who has maybe been a little below the level she showed last season and was beaten just under 20 lengths by Annie Mc at Warwick. However her course form at Cheltenham is something that will always stand to her. In six starts over fences at the track her form reads: B2212F.

The fall was this year when she exited at the second last in the Paddy Power Gold Cup, just when she was staying on, and her previous run over this distance on the New Course was an excellent second to Simply The Betts in the Brown Advisory & Merriebelle Stable Plate at the Festival last season. That run came off a mark of 149 and if she can produce a similar level of performance in this race, she'll be thereabouts, and I'd favour her over Annie Mc on that count.

Conclusion

Elimay looks a really classy mare but Shattered Love is most interesting back at the course and distance of her finest hour. She has plenty to make up with the favourite on their Naas meeting, but the rise in trip and move to Cheltenham is clearly significant, and the price differential (8/1 about Shattered Love at the time of writing) looks a little too big. Going with the course-and-distance angle, Happy Diva shouldn't be discounted given her excellent Cheltenham record. (Ronan)

Shattered Love (Happy Diva)

Index